I0820512

TITANIC

This book is dedicated to Steve Rigby of the British Titanic Society
1959–2011

Also by Richard M. Jones

The Great Gale of 1871
Lockington: Crash at the Crossing
Capsized in the Solent: The SRN6-012 Disaster
End of the Line: The Moorgate Disaster
Collision in the Night: The Sinking of HMS *Duchess*
Royal Victoria Rooms: The Rise and Fall of a Bridlington Landmark
RMS *Titanic*: The Bridlington Connections
The 50 Greatest Shipwrecks
Britain's Lost Tragedies Uncovered
The Burton Agnes Disaster
When Tankers Collide: The *Pacific Glory* Disaster
The Diary of a Royal Marine: The Life and Times of George Cutcher
The Farsley Murders
Living the Dream, Serving the Queen
Boleyn Gold (fiction)
Austen Secret (fiction)
Gunpowder Wreck (fiction)
Around the World in Shipwreck Adventures
Cretil the Cat (children's book)
Lost at Sea in Mysterious Circumstances
A to Z of Bridlington
Shipwrecks of the Solent
The Forgotten Submarine Pioneers
A-Z of Scarborough
Yorkshire Rail Disasters

TITANIC
THE SEARCHES AND THE DIVES

RICHARD M. JONES

First published in Great Britain in 2025 by
PEN AND SWORD HISTORY
An imprint of
Pen & Sword Books Ltd
Yorkshire – Philadelphia

ISBN 978 1 03612 850 0

A CIP catalogue entry for this book is available from the British Library.

Typeset in Times New Roman 12/16 by SJmagic DESIGN SERVICES, India.
Printed and bound in the UK by CPI Group (UK) Ltd.

The Publisher's authorised representative in the EU for product safety is Authorised Rep Compliance Ltd., Ground Floor, 71 Lower Baggot Street, Dublin D02 P593, Ireland. www.arccompliance.com

For a complete list of Pen & Sword titles please contact
PEN & SWORD BOOKS LIMITED
George House, Units 12 & 13, Beevor Street, Off Pontefract Road,
Barnsley, South Yorkshire, S71 1HN, England
E-mail: enquiries@pen-and-sword.co.uk
Website: www.pen-and-sword.co.uk

or

PEN AND SWORD BOOKS
1950 Lawrence Rd, Havertown, PA 19083, USA
E-mail: uspen-and-sword@casematepublishers.com
Website: www.penandswordbooks.com

CONTENTS

INTRODUCTION

A VESSEL THAT went from being a 'Ship of Dreams' to one which is synonymous with tragedy would always make headlines and spur the imagination of writers and film directors, but the fate of the liner *Titanic* has led to an unprecedented following, indeed in some cases obsession. This has seen the initial shockwaves of 1912 spread around the world like a tsunami, and the ship is still causing waves today more than a century later.

It was on 10 April 1912 that the newest and most luxurious ocean liner ever built sailed from Southampton. From that moment on, the story of the *Titanic* has been told and retold to audiences until it is so well-known that very little new evidence can be found, leading instead to ridiculous conspiracy theories about ship-swapping and coal fires causing the sinking. But the night the *Titanic* struck that iceberg led to it becoming a household name for disaster and the most famous shipwreck in history, one that has been written about in literally thousands of books and over a dozen movies.

But as the fate of the 1,500 victims led to sadness, shock and grief, the questions that were starting to be asked also led to an entire system change regarding how the rich and the poor are separated when travelling, how safety at sea cannot be compromised and also how big companies cannot simply allow their own passengers and crew to be sacrificed in the name of breaking records.

Titanic leaving Southampton in 1912.

After its launch from Belfast in 1911, the *Titanic* was almost another year in the making as the funnels and machinery were added and its staterooms made liveable for what would be some very wealthy clientele. Departing from Southampton for its maiden voyage the following year, the liner almost had a run-in with another ship that broke its moorings, leading to observers uttering tales about the ship being cursed or seeing this incident as a bad omen. But the 882.5ft-long liner stopped to anchor in Cherbourg harbour in northern France just hours later, and also anchored off Queenstown, Ireland, the following morning before finally leaving land behind.

The four days at sea were celebrated with some of the most amazing meals on a liner's menu, drinks to toast the brand-new ship, card games to entertain the gamblers amongst them and all kinds of rooms to quell the boredom of an Atlantic crossing – a library, several cafés, Turkish baths, a swimming pool and of course as much socializing as anyone could ever want. Elegant public rooms and the Grand Staircase topped by a magnificent dome would be the most memorable places that were talked about. But on the night of 14 April 1912, there was one other room that was very busy – the Marconi radio room.

Jack Phillips and Harold Bride were working hard, constantly transmitting and receiving messages by Morse code, mostly passenger chit-chat between families and businesses. However, the number of ice warnings coming from other ships in the area was also piling up, and these were mostly rushed to the bridge. *Titanic* was slightly straying off-course due to the currents pushing it south, and when an iceberg was sighted at 2340hrs on that moonless evening by the lookouts high up in the crow's nest, it came as a surprise to suddenly see this dangerous situation looming ahead.

The ship swung to port to avoid the ice, but alas it was too little too late. By the time the lookouts had seen it and action been taken, the ship had only turned enough to prevent a head-on collision and instead scraped the starboard side beneath the water line, the ice puncturing holes along the side of the ship and opening up at least five of its watertight compartments to the sea. After a brief analysis by Thomas Andrews, the liner's designer who was on board for the trip, soon calculated that the ship had just a few hours left afloat. What was worse was that the ship's lifeboats – twenty in total – would only be able to hold around half of those 2,200 people who were on board.

It took a total of two hours and forty minutes for *Titanic* to founder, and in that time the stories of that night became legendary. There were passengers like Isador and Ida Strauss, refusing to get into a lifeboat ahead of the young ones; Benjamin Guggenheim, who went down 'like a gentleman' with his valet; and Archibald Gracie, who later wrote a book on his survival, only to succumb to illnesses linked to that night before the year was out. These stories became part of *Titanic* folklore. Yet as the years went, by the story of *Titanic* faded for a time, two world wars taking the public's attention with more pressing issues.

That situation largely continued until 1955, when Walter Lord published his book on the *Titanic* named *A Night to Remember*, which encouraged the Rank Organisation to turn it into a film, one which was not only very popular but is still today in many cases seen as the most historically accurate depiction of what went on that night.

The real story of the *Titanic* was told and retold so many times that there was little that new books could add. Yet there was still a huge element to the *Titanic* saga that had not yet been covered – namely the location and condition of the wreck itself. Over the decades since the sinking there had been various news reports about serious attempts to search for the wreck of the lost liner. However, the ship lay in waters over 2 miles deep, and furthermore there were few underwater craft that could dive that deep, let alone conduct a search for the wreck.

But time and inventions started to make these far-fetched dreams a possibility. There was the development of side-scan sonar by Harold

Willy Stöwer depicts the sinking of the *Titanic* in 1912.

'Doc' Edgerton, the dive to the Mariana Trench in 1960 by the bathyscape *Trieste* (an incredible 7 miles down), the development of remotely operated vehicles that were featured on the pages of *National Geographic* magazine and explorers who had serious ambitions to chart the world's oceans for scientific purposes.

French ocean explorer and diver Jacques Cousteau made a name for himself in the 1960s and 1970s, his adventures featured on television documentaries worldwide. His converted minesweeper *Calypso* was taking them diving to some of the most incredible reefs and wrecks, firing imaginations and leading to a fascination with the underwater world. One of the things Cousteau found was the wreck of *Titanic*'s sister ship, *Britannic*, sunk by a mine in 1916 off the Greek island of Kea while serving as a hospital ship during the wartime evacuation of troops.

Although the footage was very grainy and it would be another twenty years before the next expedition to the wreck of the *Britannic*, there were already plans in place to make a search for its more famous sister. The story of the search for the wreck of the *Titanic* and the subsequent dives over the next forty years reads like a drama in itself: steeped in controversy involving allegations of grave robbing, carelessness, tragedy … and a monkey!

1

JACK GRIMM AND A MONKEY CALLED TITAN (1980)

SIXTY-EIGHT YEARS HAD passed since the tragedy of the *Titanic*. The world had seen so many changes, with two world wars and technology having gone from strength to strength. Stories of undersea exploration were making the headlines as popular magazines such as *National Geographic* took readers on adventures to the depths of the oceans with sights that had never been seen before. Images shown on TV screens seemed almost unbelievable.

With the development of deep diving submersibles, scuba equipment and side-scan sonar, it was only a matter of time before the hunt for the world's most famous lost ship would take centre stage. The wreck of the *Titanic*'s rival, *Lusitania*, sunk by a U-boat in 1915, had already been a goldmine for experimental dives in extreme conditions, but she was only a few hundred feet deep off the south coast of Ireland. With *Britannic* being discovered by Jacques Cousteau, and the availability of equipment pioneered by the Frenchman, sport diving was becoming a popular pastime that was not just for tech-savvy rich people.

Long before anyone knew the vessel's condition, there had been plans to raise the wreck of the *Titanic*, with every kind of whacky scheme, from filling the ship with ping pong balls to covering it in ice. Fiction writer Clive Cussler joined the party

Jack Grimm used the *H.J.W. Fay* on his first expedition. (US Geological Survey)

with his novel *Raise the Titanic*, later turned into a film of the same name. While the book was very popular and made the hero of the story, Dirk Pitt, a household name, the movie flopped, to the point where producer Lord Grade said it would have been 'cheaper to lower the Atlantic' with the amount of money that had been lost.

Another issue with the search for the wreck was concerns that the *Titanic* would be completely buried due to the events of 18 November 1929, when a magnitude 7.2 earthquake on the Grand Banks caused huge undersea landslides as well as twelve underwater cables to break and a tsunami to hit the coast of Newfoundland with waves up to 8 metres high. On land, the quake left twenty-eight people dead. Those intent on searching for the wreck of the *Titanic* were now concerned that the undersea landslides had buried everything in the area, including the lost wreck.

Nevertheless, fast-forward fifty years and serious expeditions to search for the *Titanic* could now be planned that were thought of as more than just a passing joke, as the technology did now exist for a scientific search for the world's most famous shipwreck. All they needed was the money to fund it, and that was where Texan oil millionaire Jack Grimm came into the story.

Born in 1925, Grimm had dreamed of treasure-hunting since he was a young boy, when he apparently detonated dynamite on a creek bed near his home in Wagoner, Oklahoma, in his search for buried artefacts. Although he found nothing of interest, it was this kind of adventure that ignited his passion for exploring further. He served in the US Marines during the Second World War as a demolition expert, then struck lucky on his first shot as a solo oil driller in Oklahoma, becoming very rich very quickly. He met a woman named Jacqueline two years after the war while studying geology, and they married and went on to have two children together. During the next few decades, he found his fortunes going down and then back up again countless times. In 1970, he joined an expedition to search for Noah's Ark on Mount Ararat in Turkey that ended with him having a small piece of wood he had dug out of the frozen mountain that he became convinced was part of the fabled ship.

Then in 1979, Grimm spoke to a Florida filmmaker named Michael Harris, who put forward a project to search for the wreck of the *Titanic*, having already made a number of programmes on the

H.J.W. Fay. (US Geological Survey)

hunt for shipwrecks in the Caribbean purportedly containing treasure from Spanish galleons. Grimm jumped at the chance and immediately set about raising the required funding, hiring the right people and gathering the equipment together in order to bring the expedition to fruition. Putting most of his own money and reputation on the table, he began to gather a team of experts.

For his 1980 expedition, Grimm hired the 175ft-long research vessel *H.J.W. Fay*, which had been originally been launched in 1966 as the *Artemis* by Jeffboat of Jeffersonville, Indiana, for survey work on oceanographic expeditions. The ship now provided up to thirty-two crew and passengers with relatively comfortable accommodation. The 545 gross ton vessel was renamed *H.J.W. Fay* in 1974 in honour of the president of the Submarine Signalling Company.

It had been sixty-eight years since the *Titanic* sank when the *H.J.W. Fay* was readied to begin the search for the wreck. Grimm was in charge of the expedition and had high hopes that he would

H.J.W. Fay. (US Geological Survey)

H.J.W. Fay. (US Geological Survey)

be successful. Up to that point, all people had done was talk about searching for the *Titanic*; he was the first person to actively start looking for it. While the *H.J.W. Fay*, owned by Tracor Marine, was a comparatively small ship, it was packed with modern equipment that Grimm believed would help him locate what remained of the liner, using sonar and a lot of patience.

Also on board were experts from the Scripps Institute of Oceanography, who almost walked off the ship before the expedition had even started when Grimm did something very bizarre that threw his integrity into question. He decided to introduce a monkey into the equation (yes, you read that right), claiming that it was 'trained' to point to places on the chart where a search for the *Titanic* should commence. The arguments that ensued showed that cooler heads had to prevail, the scientists threatening to quit the expedition unless the monkey was left on shore. Thankfully, Grimm was persuaded not to bring the monkey, which he had already christened Titan.

The ship set sail for a three-week search of the North Atlantic over the summer months of July and August 1980. From the outset,

H.J.W. Fay's bow thrusters. (US Geological Survey)

however, the expedition was plagued by terrible conditions, equipment malfunctions and teething problems with the new kit, some of which would prove worthless for a task of this magnitude. By the end of the three weeks, the results were very disappointing, the *H.J.W. Fay* returning to harbour at Port Everglades, Florida, with Grimm and his team no nearer finding the location of the wreck.

Nonetheless, newspaper reporters still published articles on the expedition, as this was still the most exciting search for the lost ship yet. Anything detailing the expedition was going to be popular for the time being. But it was soon revealed that Jack Grimm had thrown his money into many previous mad ventures: not only the hunt for Noah's Ark, but also bids to prove the existence of Big Foot and the Loch Ness Monster. Consequently, the chances of anybody really taking him seriously (especially once the monkey incident became public knowledge) were diminishing.

Never one to see events in a negative light, and despite no evidence to back up his claim, Grimm proudly announced that there was a fifty-fifty chance that he had found the *Titanic*. Whether he genuinely believed it or not, this ignited the thrill of following the story of the *Titanic* as it was genuinely believed that after so many years, there

H.J.W. Fay's mess. (US Geological Survey)

was now actually a chance that the ship would be found. Grimm said all he had to do now was return to sea to prove it – but that would be easier said than done.

Following Grimm's 1980 expedition, the *H.J.W. Fay* went back to more regular oceanic survey duties, being renamed the *Seiscom Discovery* in 1982 before becoming the *ENS 2* in January 1986, with an IMO Number of 6617659. After twenty-five years of seagoing surveys and expeditions, the vessel was finally scrapped in 1991.

The science lab on the *H.J.W. Fay*. (U.S. Geological Survey)

2

JACK GRIMM RETURNS (1981)

A YEAR HAD passed since Jack Grimm had made headlines with his search for the wreck of the *Titanic*. His failure to find anything did not alter his determination to continue with the hunt, and a year later he hired a 182ft research vessel named the *Gyre* for another expedition.

The *Gyre* was built by Halter Marine Services Inc of New Orleans for the United States Navy, and was launched on 23 May 1973, being delivered to the Navy on 14 November of that year, the lead ship of a class of AGOR-21 research vessels. At 798 gross tons, the *Gyre* was a state-of-the-art ship, with hydraulic electric bow thrusters, both wet and dry laboratories (with space for an instrument van on the deck), two A-frames that could raise and lower equipment over the side of the vessel and a number of winches to assist with all of these tasks and more.

The ship could operate with five officers, five crew and twenty-three scientists, who could be sustained at sea for around sixty days, with a cruising speed of 9.5 knots (and a maximum of 11.8 knots if required). Its dark red hull and white superstructure sported twin funnels, side-by-side, and every part looked like it had an important purpose for an expedition, yet it seemed squat in comparison to other ships, the bridge being only two decks high.

Gyre around the time of Jack Grimm's second Titanic expedition. (Author)

Yet this ship was at the forefront of the next part of the *Titanic* story when Grimm set sail to the search area in June 1981 with a new determination that he would be the one to locate the wreck. He was so confident that he was close to achieving his goal that he believed he was guaranteed to produce results. The survey ship arrived at the location where Grimm believed the *Titanic* lay and immediately got to work scanning the search area. However, one-by-one, his target areas were located and then discounted. Despite these setbacks, he was convinced that a strange-looking shape seen on the seabed could only be the blade of one of the *Titanic*'s propellers, proudly announcing this to be so when the ship returned to port in Boston. The 'propeller' then became his obsession as people watched and listened from the sidelines to find out what he would do next.

This expedition had cost him around £500,000, and all he had to show for it was scientists dismissing the 'propeller' find as inconclusive – and they would be right. They had spent ten days scanning around 60 miles of seabed, using a range of sonar, magnetometer and underwater cameras, but despite Grimm's confidence, everyone else seemed less convinced by what he claimed they had found. He now had to prove it once and for all, beginning to plan a third trip out into the Atlantic.

Meanwhile, the *Gyre* continued its work for the US Navy, having a major rebuild in 1984 before being sold to Texas A&M University in August 1992. Its new owners ran a number of surveys out of Galveston, one large project in 2000 seeing it at sea for 194 days on fifteen cruises. Numerous reports and papers were published regarding its findings, although each year it was costing a staggering $1.37 million to run the vessel, including fuel, crew and general maintenance. By July 2005, it was decided to retire the *Gyre*, much to the sadness of those who had served on board. This left the university's oceanography department without a research ship for the first time in fifty years. For one of the crew, this meant retirement after spending thirty-one years on board as a mate, telling the *Houston Chronicle* that he had no regrets and had seen some amazing places during his time on the *Gyre*.

Yet this was not the end of the road for the *Gyre*, which had a new lease of life when it was purchased by TDI-Brooks International Inc in 2005. Since then, it has been hard at work back out at sea. Registered in the Pacific islands of Vanuatu since 2014, the *Gyre* is still going strong at the time of writing, performing offshore geochemical exploration, underwater inspections and pipeline damage assessments.

TDI-Brooks operate the *Gyre* (IMO Number 7318999) along with three other vessels and advertise themselves as providing 'Scientific Services on a Global Basis', offering their ships and crew for hire for jobs such as that which Grimm undertook more than four decades ago. Their main area of operation is the mid-Atlantic, around the northern part of South America, Mexico and North/West Africa, as well as the Mediterranean. At the forefront of their advertising is that safety is paramount to their operations, with all vessels regularly vetted by

Gyre today, still surveying the oceans. (TDI Brooks International)

client marine assurance groups and being part of the Offshore Vessel Inspection Database.

Back in 1981, as Jack Grimm pondered his 'propeller' conundrum, he was planning a third expedition. This time he was even more confident that he would prove once and for all where the sunken *Titanic* now lay.

3

JACK GRIMM AND HIS PROPELLER (1983)

IT WOULD BE another two years before Jack Grimm made a return to the North Atlantic in his final quest for the elusive wreck. With two expeditions under his belt and nothing concrete to say he had achieved anything more than finding out where the *Titanic* wasn't resting, Grimm found his next survey ship, once again courtesy of the US Navy.

Laid down in January 1961, the oceanographic research vessel *Robert D. Conrad* was 209ft long and weighed 1,072 gross tons. Built by Gibbs Systems Inc. in Jacksonville, Florida, it was owned by the US Navy and named after one of their officers who had served on both sides of the Atlantic during the Second World War before he retired in 1947 and died two years later. The ship now bearing his name was launched on 26 May 1962 by Mrs Edmund B. Taylor and entered service in November that year. The single-screw vessel was diesel-electric powered and had a white hull, blue funnel and two masts, with the ability to carry an array of modern technology. Up to thirty-eight scientists and twenty-three crew could live comfortably at sea for weeks at a time. The first of three Robert D. Conrad-class ships, its two sister ships were the *Thomas G. Thompson* and *Thomas Washington*. Like the *Gyre*, the *Robert D. Conrad* had wet and dry laboratories, photo labs and the ability to lower equipment over the side to perform scientific duties – perfect to search for a deep-water shipwreck.

For its first role as a new ship, it was tasked with assisting the Lamont Geological Observatory at Columbia University, along with two other ships, for oceanographic work with the Office of Naval Research, providing seismic data, taking core samples as well as mapping the seabed. The ship performed well and would go on to be a workhorse for Columbia's science teams for many years to come.

In 1963, after the loss of submarine USS *Thresher* in mysterious circumstances, the *Robert D. Conrad* was part of the group that was tasked to search for the wreck in the hope of finding out what went wrong and how 129 people met their deaths (the story of this submarine wreck would play a part in the *Titanic* story several years

Jack Grimm returned to the Atlantic using the *Robert D. Conrad.* (USN 1065688)

later). Surveys were carried out of the area where the submarine went down, with a lot of data accumulated for the investigation teams, but this would not be the last expedition to this wreck site.

Further seabed survey work carried out by the *Robert D. Conrad* led to major breakthroughs in how scientists understand seafloor spreading, and the ship became only the second-ever vessel to carry out over a million nautical miles of oceanographic research.

In July 1983, it was back at sea again, this time with Jack Grimm on board for his third *Titanic* expedition, convinced that this would be the one that confirmed his theory that his propeller belonged to the lost liner. Grimm was also hoping that this would be the expedition that would prove that the images he had looked at two years before were part of the wreck, as he had claimed. The *Robert D. Conrad* set sail and headed to the search area, Grimm filled with confidence and enthusiasm.

Alas, Grimm was once again unsuccessful. He could not prove that any wreckage had been found, and he came home empty-handed after several weeks at sea. Following the failure of his third expedition, he never tried to search for the *Titanic* again. Ironically, when the wreck was eventually found, it was proved that he had come very close to it on more than one occasion; perhaps he may have located it himself if it wasn't for the weather slowing him down or if he had gone back out one last time. However, Grimm would always be known as the man who failed to find the wreck of the *Titanic*, his reputation not helped by the notorious monkey incident.

The *Robert D. Conrad* (IMO Number 7742140) was eventually laid up on the James River in Virginia from July 1989 and was retired from the US Navy on 4 October 1989, when it was finally struck off the Navy List. The vessel was sold for breaking up in November 2003 at Bay Bridge Enterprises in Chesapeake, Virginia, and its scrapping was completed by the end of April 2004.

Along with William Hoffman, Jack Grimm published *Beyond Reach – The Search for the Titanic* in 1982, documenting his first expedition and sealing his name forever in the story of the doomed liner. Grimm died of cancer at the age of 72 on 6 January 1998, having always insisted that he had actually found the *Titanic* on his three expeditions, as well as claiming the title of discoverer of Noah's Ark on Mount Ararat in Turkey. His wife died in 2003 and was buried alongside Jack in Abilene, Texas. They left behind two children, four grandchildren and a great grandchild.

4

FRENCH-AMERICAN COLLABORATION (1985)

WITH JACK GRIMM bowing out as the only serious contender in the search for the legendary *Titanic*, it was left to other explorers to carry on the search, inspired by his lead. Dr Robert Ballard was one of these explorers. Born in 1943 and raised in Kansas, Ballard's love of the oceans and checking out the rock pools around the beaches led him to pursue oceanography as a career. After doing service with the US Navy, he soon found himself on board a variety of research vessels, taking up a position with the Woods Hole Oceanographic Institution at Cape Cod, Massachusetts. Here, his love of the sea proved that he had chosen the right path in life. He was soon diving on sea life that nobody had ever seen while pioneering new technologies that saw the first amazing images of underwater volcanoes (known as Black Smokers), hydrothermal vents that were so hot they could melt lead. Living besides these powerful and dangerous features were newly discovered tube worms, giant clams and all kinds of other life that was dependent on the chemicals in the water to survive and not the sun, this completely rewriting everything that was known about wildlife on Earth being dependent on the sun for survival.

As the years passed by, Ballard found his name in *National Geographic* magazine several times. In 1983, he published the excellent book *Exploring Our Living Planet*, in which he explained many of the discoveries that he had been involved with and how important it was to explore the oceans and find answers to the deep-sea mysteries along the way.

After having a chat to a man named Bill Tatum from the Titanic Historical Society, Ballard's mind wondered at the thought of actually having the technology to be able to dive to the wreck of the *Titanic*. Of course it would first have to be located, over 2 miles down, where few submersibles could reach (*Trieste* had broken all records in 1960 by diving to the Mariana Trench around 7 miles down). Then the Woods Hole submersible *Alvin* had a refit and its maximum depth capability was doubled to around that at which *Titanic*'s wreck was thought to lay. That got his mind fired up, and soon he was making enquiries as to whether this was a project that was feasible.

Ballard had contacts within the US Navy and discussions began about testing a whole array of new search equipment. Before long he had secured a deal to carry out work for them using their latest technology, with the promise that he could use the remaining days left on the expedition to use the kit to hunt for the *Titanic*. This was only part of the project; he would never find it in just a few days, so he needed another team working in the search area while he was conducting the work for the Navy. This was where the French oceanographic organization IFREMER came along (the Institut Français de Recherche pour l'Exploitation de la Mer, the French Research Institute for Exploration of the Sea, based in the French port of Brest).

They got together this second team to make a joint French-American expedition, IFREMER bringing in their research vessel *Le Suroit* (IMO number 7360368) to start their end of the search area. Built for them in 1975 at Ateliers et Chantiers de la Manche in Dieppe, northern France, the ship weighed 946 gross tons and was 184.8ft long, and had already carried out a number of successful expeditions at sea for the institute, whose main aim was scientific research of the oceans, coasts, wildlife and ecosystems. It was in the summer of

The French side of the 1985 search used the research ship *Le Suroît*. (Julien 1978)

1985 that *Le Suroit* was tasked with its most famous mission yet – the first round in another search for the *Titanic*.

Conducting phase one of the *Titanic* seabed survey, the French team used a torpedo-shaped sonar device called SAR (Sonar Acoustique Remorque) that could be lowered from the stern A-frame to scan the seabed over 2 miles below to give a large area sweep. Any anomaly would show up on the computer screens back in the control room, and if any of these targets looked promising, a visual check with cameras could be used later to confirm or refute its identity.

Leading this part of the expedition was Jean-Louis Michel, and for ten days the survey ship criss-crossed the Atlantic search area, as had the Grimm expeditions in previous years. Also like Grimm, the *Le Suroit* actually came very close to the wreck, although until the location of the *Titanic* was confirmed, none of them knew this. On 6 August, the French team's job was completed and the baton was passed to Ballard on board the American vessel *Knorr*, the *Le Suroit* turning for home. It would soon become apparent just how close they had been.

Following its return to port, *Le Suroit* went back to work on scientific expeditions, conducting ocean surveys and seabed mapping

Le Suroît alongside in Concarneau, Brittany. (Jean-Baptiste Fagot (Cyberugo))

using new computer software that has changed the understanding of our seas. Based in Brest, it was one of over a dozen vessels that IFREMER used on a daily basis to help increase knowledge of the oceans, inspiring new generations of explorers along the way.

By 2021, however, *Le Suroit* was showing its age and was sold on, being renamed *Grand Nord*, registered in Panama. Although its name was changed, the outline of the former name and the IFREMER symbols down the side of the hull could still be seen under a thin layer of paint. It was last known of in Gdansk, Poland, listed as a cargo vessel, its official status being simply 'decommissioned'.

Back in the summer of 1985, with the French side of the search expedition over, attention was now focused on what Ballard was about to do. And the clock was ticking.

5

DISCOVERY (1985)

SAILING OUT INTO the Atlantic in the summer of 1985, Robert Ballard was heading to the site of his latest mission aboard the research vessel *Knorr*. Launched by the Defoe Shipbuilding Company of Bay City, Michigan, on 21 August 1968, the vessel was placed under operational control to the Woods Hole Oceanographic Institution and delivered on 15 April 1970 for oceanographic research purposes. Named after US Navy hydrographic engineer and cartographer Ernest Knorr for his work between 1860 and 1885, the ship was fitted with cycloidal propulsion with both bow and stern thrusters, and could hover over a site with ease while scientists and engineers worked on a specific seabed position. The ship could carry a crew of twenty-two while hosting thirty-two scientists, and had a variety of upper-deck equipment that allowed a range of survey vehicles to be lowered over the side, purpose-built control rooms being set up to monitor the video screens. With a sleek blue hull and single funnel, *Knorr* (IMO Number 7738618) was 279ft long and had a gross tonnage of 2,518.

But it was not the *Titanic* wreck site that Ballard was heading to right now, his deal with the US Navy meaning that he was tasked with a mission to survey two completely different wrecks of high importance. These were two US Navy nuclear submarines that had been lost with all hands in the 1960s, and the military wanted to know more about the condition of their wreck sites and if there was any further evidence regarding the cause of their demise.

The *Knorr* headed east, out into the Atlantic. On board were the camera sleds named *Argo* and *ANGUS* (Acoustically Navigated Geological Underwater Survey), which would be lowered into the sea and down to the ocean floor via miles of cable. These would bring back live images of the wreckage once they were on site, which could be recorded and photographed via the screens within the control room. This whole mission was top secret; at no point was Ballard to reveal the real reason why his *Titanic* expedition was going ahead.

The location of the two submarines was known, so *Knorr* sailed direct to each site without any issues. The USS *Thresher* had failed to surface following a set of trials on 9 April 1963, all 129 crew being lost. Five years later, on 22 May 1968, the USS *Scorpion* was heading to observe Russian naval activity in the Atlantic and suddenly went silent; it carried a crew of ninety-nine. Ballard's team filmed the twisted wreckage of the two submarines, which littered the cold Atlantic seabed many hundreds of miles apart. While it was clear that *Thresher* had imploded by going too deep, the cause of the *Scorpion* disaster has never been determined. Ballard spent several weeks carefully lowering *Argo* and criss-crossing the seabed, photographing and filming the wreckage. The expedition got the job done, bringing back footage of the broken pieces of the stricken submarines.

Once these survey jobs were complete, the *Knorr* headed towards the *Titanic* search area, ready to take over from *Le Suroit*. By now, the search for *Titanic* was up against a tight deadline; they had less than two weeks to get a result. With his French colleagues not having anything to show for their time there (again, other than where *Titanic* wasn't), Ballard was starting to have doubts about the search positions and the very real fear that *Titanic* was not where it had reported it was in 1912. Settling into a twenty-four-hour watch system, the team once again lowered *Argo* into position and watched a live TV feed of the seabed. The theory was that whenever a ship sinks to that kind of depth, there would be a scattering of light debris, which would lead to the heavier items closer to the wreck itself. The second part of the expedition started with just empty seabed, carrying on like this for many days. The monotony of staring at the screens and seeing nothing became a routine of boring hours and endless days. With the *Knorr* slowly moving along at a maximum speed of around 2 knots, the crew settled in for the tedious checking of equipment and watching the monitors for any sign of man-made material. At such times, the mind could play tricks on people, convincing them that they had seen something out of the ordinary, but it was just a shadow on a muddy mound, a sea creature or a blur on the screen. The quiet of the control room would be occasionally shattered by the printer or the moving of a chair as hour after hour passed without anything new to report.

Then suddenly, in the early morning of 1 September 1985, the cameras from *Argo* picked up what looked like man-made objects. Was this the first wreckage from *Titanic*'s debris field? After countless soul-destroying hours looking at nothing, there were shouts of joy from team members, feeling that perhaps the expedition had after all been a success. More and more debris came into view, and hopes were raised that they had indeed located the wreckage of the *Titanic*. Yet it quickly became a sombre moment, as the understanding sank in of what had happened at this exact spot so many years ago. Ballard called a memorial service in the stern of the *Knorr*, where the team paused to remember the 1,500 lives lost here at almost the same cold dark hour of the night back in April 1912. After this short pause, it was back to work with the hunt for the main wreckage of the lost liner. All hoped it would now only be a matter of time before the hulk emerged. The first clue that they had definitely located the *Titanic* came with the image of one of the huge boilers appearing on their screens, with the three closed doors looking directly at the camera. This was one of sixteen boilers that had been lowered into position when the ship was built in Belfast;

it had broken loose when *Titanic* lifted its stern into the air on the night of the sinking.

As the cameras passed over more seabed and pieces of wreckage, the broken and rusting hull of the wreck of the *Titanic* finally came into view on *Argo*'s cameras, the first time anyone had gazed upon it since the ship had sunk seventy-three years ago. Revelations started to come in thick and fast: the funnels were gone; only half of the ship was there (it turned out that the other section was over a thousand feet away); the mast had collapsed down onto the bridge area – which itself was now gone; and the crow's nest – where Frederick Fleet and Reginald Lee had spotted the approaching iceberg that fateful night – was still visible. Over the next few days, the first images of the main hull of the *Titanic* were captured in the still and video shots that were now being produced. Right up until the last moment, teams were working hard to get pictures that were good enough to show to the world's press when they returned to port.

As word arrived ashore of the discovery, the press went into a frenzy. Ballard found himself spending much of his time on the phone to news agencies and television news stations. This was magnified when *Knorr* returned to port at Cape Cod in Massachusetts, the ship and those aboard received a hero's welcome. A press conference was called, at which Ballard stood in front of the world's media

A later image of the *Knorr* in Greenland in 2011. (Sindre Skrede)

Robert Ballard's research vessel *Knorr*. (BenFrantzDale)

and spoke of the success of the expeditions; but for him, this was just the beginning. At the age of 42, he was now officially the man who discovered of the wreck of the *Titanic*. But he was almost immediately planning a second expedition to obtain better and more closely detailed footage of the *Titanic*. In the meantime, the enormity of his discovery and the fact that a dreadful disaster had occurred right where he had just been hit Ballard harder than he had expected. For many months, he could not bring himself talk any more about the discovery, choosing instead to focus on his work and making plans for the following year's survey.

For the research vessel *Knorr*, it would be back to normality with ocean survey and exploration jobs to be carried out, the workhorse of Woods Hole continuing to transport scientists to the site of some of the most amazing discoveries known to man. However, nothing would top the discovery of the most famous shipwreck in history.

The *Knorr* received several refits over the coming years, with many additions such as a strengthened bow to cut through ice and the ability to retrieve 150ft core samples from the seabed, as well as a new dynamic positioning system that allowed the vessel to move wherever it was programmed to, facilitating the needs of scientists requiriing a stable platform. After almost forty-five years working for the Woods Hole Oceanographic Institution, it was announced on 4 December 2014 that the *Knorr* would be decommissioned, and two years later the vessel started a new career with the Mexican Navy, renamed as *Rio Tecolutla*. In the month before the final handover to its new owners, a number of crew members were on board to conduct training with the outgoing crew, with further additions to be placed on board once the ship had arrived in its new home port. The famous research ship was officially handed over in a ceremony held on board the *Knorr* involving the US Navy and the naval attaché at the Mexican Embassy. The Mexican flag was hoisted and the new crew, along with a number of guests, toasted the ship's new career while celebrated its past exploits. At the time of writing, the *Rio Tecolutla* was still in service.

6

RETURN TO THE *TITANIC* (1986)

FOLLOWING HIS SUCCESS with the discovery of the *Titanic*, Dr Robert Ballard wanted to bring the world some better footage of the wreck. He knew that he needed to make a manned dive to the site to conduct the first proper survey so he could answer some of the thousands of questions that were now being asked. The world was eager to learn more about the state of the wreck. The images obtained so far of *Titanic* were very limited, not showing enough of the wreck to reveal just what state it was in. With Ballard clearly intending to head back, the exact location was for now kept a strictly guarded secret. In the summer of 1986, the 210ft-long research vessel *Atlantis II* was put at Ballard's disposal, enabling him to make his second expedition to the wreck site.

Built by the Maryland Shipbuilding and Drydock Company for the Woods Hole Oceanographic Institution as a research platform for deep-water exploration, *Atlantis II* was named in tribute to Woods Hole's original ketch, *Atlantis*, which was launched in 1930 (and after several name changes is at the time of writing still around today in Argentina). The second ship to bear this name was launched on 8 September 1962, and at 1,701 gross tons began its long and illustrious career on 1 February the following year. Its sleek blue hull was fitted with a winch on the fantail in order to launch large submersibles for manned dives on geological sites. A team of twenty-five scientists could work closely with the ship's

Stuart Williamson painting of the bow section of *Titanic* as Ballard first saw it. (Stuart Williamson)

crew of thirty-three to conduct expeditions lasting weeks at a time in conditions that would leave many other survey ships heading back to port.

As *Atlantis II* now sailed into the Atlantic, resting on its stern was a submersible that had already made headlines. The 17-ton *Alvin* was built in 1964 by General Mills Electronic Group of Minnesota as a tool of exploration for the US Navy. It was operated by Woods Hole Oceanographic Institute with the aim of furthering the understanding of the world's oceans. At 23ft 4in long, little did anyone foresee just what a colourful and varied career *Alvin* would have.

The submersible was designed around a sphere, into which three people could squeeze and sit, peering out of small viewports. The whole sphere could be completely detached from the rest of the unit in the event of an emergency. At the front of the view ports were manipulator arms, allowing samples to be carefully grabbed and placed into a tray, to be examined when the sub reached the surface.

Just a year after *Alvin*'s first launch, on 17 January 1966, a mid-air collision off the Spanish coast between a refuelling tanker and a B-52G bomber of the US Air Force left seven dead and four hydrogen bombs missing. The first three bombs were found on land, but the fourth was lost at sea and a huge search operation was launched to locate and recover it as quickly as possible. This is where *Alvin* came in.

Diving off the coast of Spain looking for a hydrogen bomb, with the eyes of the world watching, made those on the expedition nervous. Questions were raised by the press over the safety of the bomb and whether it could even be located. It took two months of seabed searching, using a number of underwater cameras, before the

Alvin on the surface with *Atlantis II* in the background. (NOAA)

bomb was finally located by *Alvin*, some 2,990ft deep. The bomb was raised intact on 7 April, leading to celebrations all around for a job well done.

A year later, a random incident occurred that led to the submersible having to declare an emergency. On 6 July 1967, *Alvin* was on a dive at 2,000ft when a swordfish swam close by and took a keen interest in the deep-sea intruder. The fish decided to attack the sub and got its long bill jammed in the hull, the crew having to initiate an emergency ascent. Upon arriving at the surface, the offending fish was removed from the submersible and later eaten by the crew of the support ship.

Another year went by without incident, then on 16 October 1968, *Alvin* was being launched for a regular dive from the support vessel *Lulu*, a procedure that had happened hundreds of times over the last few years, when suddenly the cables holding *Alvin* in place snapped and the sub sunk to the seabed. Thankfully, the three crew members managed to get clear before the sub sank, with one suffering minor injuries. The sub would remain on the floor of the ocean, almost 5,000ft down, until August the following year, when it was salvaged and repaired. When the salvage took place, the crew's packed lunch from the day of the accident was not only preserved but actually still edible after some ten months at the bottom of the sea.

Alvin was soon back on the Mid-Atlantic Ridge, exploring hydrothermal vents on what was known as Project FAMOUS (French American Mid-Ocean Undersea Survey). Each time the expeditions brought back new and incredible finds, images of *Alvin* on the seabed adorned the pages of science magazines as well as *National Geographic*. This was an incredible time to be a deep-ocean explorer, as Robert Ballard had already found out, this being in the days before he dived on *Titanic*.

When *Alvin* was fitted out with a new titanium sphere, allowing it to descend a lot deeper than before, Ballard believed that it would be perfect to explore the *Titanic* wreck site as it should be able to handle the 12,000ft depth. In July 1986, using *Atlantis II* as the control ship,

Alvin in its hangar aboard *Atlantis II*. (NOAA)

Alvin first visited the wreck of the submarine USS *Scorpion*, then Ballard's team continued on to the *Titanic* wreck site. He anticipated a three-week expedition to explore what remained of the most famous ship in the world.

On the first dive, technical issues meant it took over two hours to descend to the seabed only to have the dive cut short, meaning that after seeing the hull of the stricken liner for literally a few seconds, the dive had to be aborted. Nevertheless, later dives brought back incredible images, from both inside and outside of the wreck. The crew on *Atlantis II* were astounded by the condition of the remains of the ship, the vastness of the debris field and the latest pictures that were coming in thick and fast revealing areas of the ship that had not been seen for over seven decades. The condition of *Titanic*'s two halves were very different: the bow was very much intact, although the funnels were gone and the bridge had been swept away, but the

Alvin being raised out of the water by *Atlantis II*. (NOAA)

stern had ended up a complete mess. Was this because of the speed of the wreck hitting the seabed, or had trapped air caused an implosion? At the time, there were more questions than answers.

On board *Alvin*, tucked away at the front in a tiny cage, was a Remotely Operated Vehicle (ROV) named *Jason Junior* (*JJ* for short), a small blue contraption that had lights, cameras and thrusters, facilitating a video feed to the controller in the submersible. With *Alvin* set down at a safe location, *JJ* would be launched and carefully guided into hard-to-reach places such as the Grand Staircase, where its cameras picked up a chandelier hanging from its wire, the staircase itself and the ornate Honour and Glory clock being long gone.

When the final dive was completed, the treasure trove of video footage and still images were lapped up by a world hungry for the results of the first manned dive to the wreck of the *Titanic*. Before the expedition left the site, Ballard placed a plaque on the stern of the wreck, the last place where those who were fighting for their lives gathered as the ship slipped beneath the waves seventy-four years beforehand. The plaque both commemorates the loss of life and recognizes the discovery of *Titanic*'s last resting place:

> 'In memory of those souls who perished with the "Titanic" April 14/15 1912. Dedicated to William H. Tantum, IV whose dream to find the "Titanic" has been realized by Dr Robert D. Ballard. The officers and members of the Titanic Historical Society Inc, 1986.'

A second plaque from The Explorers Club was placed on top of a capstan at the bow section. *Alvin* then made its final ascent from the wreck and was hoisted back on board the support ship.

Returning to Cape Cod, *Atlantis II* was greeted by a phalanx of press reporters eager to know what the *Titanic* was like. The focus was on the footage that was released and the images that found their way into newspapers and magazines around the world.

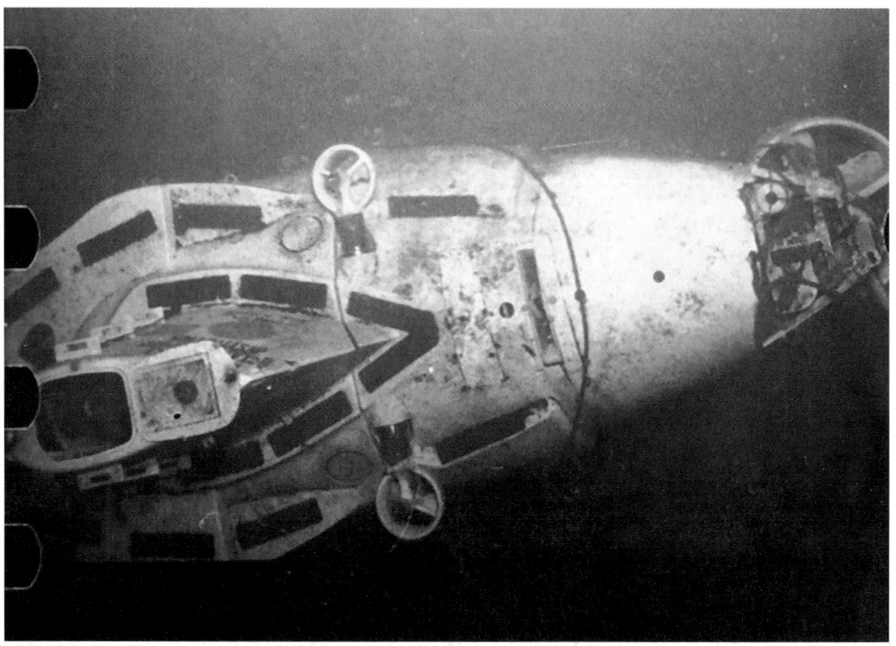

Alvin after it sank in 1968. It would be a year before it was raised again. (Office of Naval Research)

Ballard's book *The Discovery of the Titanic* was a worldwide bestseller, cementing the name *Atlantis II* into the annals of history. In the meantime, the research vessel returned to other expeditions. The ship went back out to sea and carried on with its scientific work. The name of the vessel was given to two features which it discovered on the seafloor – the Atlantis II Seamounts in the Atlantic and the Atlantis II Fracture Zone in the Indian Ocean.

Atlantis II was sold in 1996 to a private company and underwent two name changes; in 1997 it became the *Antares*, then in 1999 it was renamed *Atlantic Vision*. Later in 1999 it reverted to *Atlantis II*, but was languishing idle in New Orleans, in which state it would remain for ten years. As the vessel was about to be sent for scrapping, travel company Outlander Expeditions purchased it in 2006 and began refitting it to be able to get back to sea. It was rechristened in the

Alvin. (NOAA)

Bahamas on 18 July 2007 and returned to Woods Hole for a visit, much to the delight of those who remembered the vessel and had fond memories of trips on board. *Atlantis II* (IMO Number 5029752) was still going strong in 2025, once again performing the role that it had been designed for over sixty years ago.

Stuart Williamson's model shows the area around the broken first funnel and bridge of *Titanic*. (Stuart Williamson)

As for *Alvin*, it is the most famous underwater vehicle in the world. A book, *The Water Baby*, was written about its career, and Woods Hole sent it on numerous expeditions around the globe, including the site of the 2010 *Deepwater Horizon* disaster to check on damage to the seafloor following the catastrophic explosion, fire and oil spill that devastated parts of the Gulf of Mexico.

At the time of writing, *Alvin* was still going, the new research vessel *Atlantis* (launched in 1996) being its support ship. It continues

Titanic wreck bow railings. (NOAA)

to explore and record inaccessible parts of the world with remarkable clarity, and while ever there is ocean to explore and life left in the old sub, *Alvin* will be there to bring back footage and open up new realms of mystery. Unfortunately for *JJ*, the ROV was lost in the sinking of a barge during an expedition to the Galapagos Islands in 1991.

Robert Ballard hoped that the *Titanic* would now be left alone, a museum on the seabed where submersibles could occasionally visit, a moment in time preserved just as it had been over seventy years before. What he did not want was for the wreck site to be disturbed by treasure hunters or salvage teams. He would be sorely disappointed.

7

THE FIRST SALVAGE (1987)

WHILE BALLARD AND WOODS HOLE were adamant that the position of the wreck of the *Titanic* should be kept a secret, their co-finders at IFREMER had other ideas. It was not long before an expedition was launched, funded by the group Titanic Ventures LP, to do exactly what Ballard was against – recover items from the wreck site and bring them to the surface. To do this, they needed a state-of-the-art ship and submersible – enter the research vessel *Nadir* and submersible *Nautile*.

The 184ft-long *Nadir* was built by Ateliers & Chantiers Auroux at Arcachon, France, in 1974 for IFREMER. Weighing 1,142 gross tons, it was large enough to carry the *Nautile* and conduct numerous launches, along with a fair amount of space around the ship to store any salvaged items. An on-board team would be able to carefully begin the process of preserving finds until they were brought back to France for conservation.

The yellow submersible *Nautile* is just 26.2ft long and weighs 19.5 tons, launched – like *Alvin* – from a crane on the stern of the mother ship. It was built specifically for the French oceanographic organization IFREMER, and has since its launch in 1984 succeeded in a multitude of large-scale expeditions that have resulted in major investigations being carried out based on the evidence it collected. Armed with a number of both still and video cameras, floodlights and manipulator arms, and with its name emblazoned down the side in

A 1987 expedition patch. (Scott Caldwell)

large letters, *Nautile* can dive down to 20,000ft and remain on station for up to eight hours with three crew members in the cab. Being one of only a few manned submersibles available in 1987, it was selected to partake in the *Titanic* salvage dives

In July 1987, *Nadir* set sail under a cloud of controversy over the moral issue of taking items from the site of a disaster. Many people, including *Titanic* survivors and their relatives, accused the salvage teams of grave robbing, the equivalent of desecrating a tomb. But the expedition still went ahead, carrying out a total of thirty-two dives in the *Nautile* and bringing to the surface over 1,800 objects

The submersible *Nautile*, which carried out the first salvage dives in 1987. (Jean-François Rees)

over a seven-week period. Among the finds they raised were various personal items, leading to further outrage. There was a decorative cherub from one of the staircases, instruments from the area of the Docking Bridge and a leather travel bag. To show the world what was going on under the sea and where the artefacts were heading once they reached the surface, the team created a television documentary, *Return to the Titanic (Live from Paris)*, which was broadcast on 28 October 1987 and hosted by *Kojak* star Telly Savalas. Despite the protests, in all fairness to the salvage teams, the items were genuinely cared for. They would eventually be put on display in travelling exhibitions around the world.

The expedition ended and *Nadir* returned to port, where the artefacts were unloaded and taken away to be conserved. As all the other non-*Titanic* IFREMER expeditions became more sophisticated, their ships became newer and more advanced, meaning *Nadir* was soon showing its age and was later sold. In 2005, the ship was renamed *Deepocean Quest*, then becoming the *Alucia* in June the following year. After a complete rebuild in 2008, it is now looks very different to how it did during its *Titanic* salvage days, being renamed the *Odyssey* (IMO Number 7347823) in 2022. Officially classed as a private yacht under the flag of the Marshall Islands, its new owners are making sure *Nadir* is still sailing the seas to this day.

As for the *Nautile*, the *Titanic* was not the only shipwreck that it was to dive. On 19 November 2002, the oil tanker *Prestige* broke apart off the coast of Spain and sank with a cargo of 77,000 tons of heavy fuel oil, which was mostly in storage tanks on the seabed, leading to an environmental disaster with the fuel leaking out and the potential for these tanks to break apart. It was decided to conduct a full survey of the wreck, which was laying upright on the ocean floor at a depth of 2 miles. *Nautile* was launched over the wreck site in

The IFREMER research vessel *Nadir* (seen here at Great Yarmouth). (Gary Markham)

December of that year; it not only conducted the survey of the hull, but used its robotic arms to seal up a number of holes where fuel was seen leaking into the sea, using a variety of plugs and bungs. Despite the huge amount of oil already spilled, salvage teams were able to remove some oil from the wreck and have it taken away, reducing the impact of any future leaks.

Fast forward to 2009 and Air France flight 447, an Airbus A330-203, crashes into the sea on a flight from Rio de Janeiro to Paris. There were no survivors from the 228 people on board. Wreckage was spotted a day later by a search aircraft, and the hunt for the cause of the disaster began. The French research vessel *Pourquoi Pas?* brought the *Nautile* to the site of the wreckage, where the submersible began the hunt for the aircraft's black box flight recorders while scanning the seabed for clues as to why a modern jet would suddenly crash. Although *Nautile* was not successful in the search for the two recorders (they were found almost two years later), the sub was still fundamental to the combined search effort of a number of French and American units working together.

Needless to say, the *Nautile* is still going strong today. A replica of it is on display in Cherbourg's maritime museum, giving an idea of its size. It is one of the most famous submersibles in the world.

As for the *Titanic* treasures, the photographs that were later released showing these remarkable items and their state of preservation spurred a number of newspaper and magazine special editions and pull-outs that wowed readers and provided an insight into what was found, raised and catalogued from the wreck. These special editions are today valued by collectors around the world.

8

THE IMAX EXPEDITION (1991)

THE EARLY 1990s saw the Russians get involved with the *Titanic* in a surprising way, forming a large part of an expedition in 1991 using the 400ft research vessel *Akademik Mstislav Keldysh* (IMO Number 7811018), more commonly simply referred to as the *Keldysh*.

Named after Mstislav Vsevolodovich Keldysh (1911–1978), a Soviet mathematician and engineer of their space programme, the ship that went on to bear his name was launched from the builders yard at Hollming Oy in Fauma, Finland, on 28 December 1980 as a purpose-built science and research ship for the Russian Academy of Science. It was intended to show the world that the Russians were a world leader in the pursuit of knowledge and ocean science, and in the case of this ship at least, they have been successful.

At 6,240 gross tons and with forty-five crew on board and the same number of scientists, the *Keldysh*'s major turning point came in 1987 when it became the mother ship for two brand-new 26ft-long submersibles named *Mir 1* and *Mir 2*. Built at Rauma-Repola Oceanics, Lokomo, Finland, the two 18.6-ton subs were partnered with the *Keldysh* and swiftly became synonymous with ocean exploration.

Named after the Russian word for 'peace', the two *Mir*s were built in 1987 and designed to dive to a depth of 20,000ft, each carrying a crew of three. The subs were able to work alongside each other to in theory get any job done in half the time, support ship *Keldysh* launching them from specially designed bays on either side of the upper deck under protective canopies.

Although white in colour, their top is a bright orange so that when they surface they can easily be seen, hooked up and hoisted back on board. These two subs often surface in the dark after spending all day on the seabed, a rigid inflatable boat simply hooking them up to the support ship by the use of a 'jumper' who would leap on board to connect the cord. While underwater, a set of powerful lights can extend either side of the viewports to illuminate the target area for better footage on the video feed.

In April 1989, Soviet nuclear submarine *Komsomolets* suffered a fire and then sank in the Arctic Ocean. The *Keldysh* was tasked to help search for the wreck, a mission that was successfully accomplished two months later. Two later expeditions were carried out by *Keldysh* using the *Mir* submersibles to help plug holes in the hull after radiation concerns were raised, leading to a documentary crew highlighting the plight of Russia's nuclear submarines that were then laying rotten in ports after their useful lives had come to an end. The dives on the wreck of the *Komsomolets* showed to the world the dangers of leaving these wrecks on the seabed with their nuclear weapons and active reactors on board.

Dr Joe MacInnis was a Canadian undersea physician who had already been on several *Titanic* dives, being part of the original team that located the wreck in 1985. He planned to make further dives to the wreck in order to conduct geological and biological studies of the site, as well as to film the *Titanic* in a way that had never been done before.

In 1991, MacInnis and the IMAX Corporation mounted an expedition to the *Titanic* using the *Mir*s to film the wreck using powerful lights and cameras, capturing images of the liner to be projected onto huge purpose-built screens in IMAX theatres.

The expedition got underway and the teams soon found themselves descending some 2½ miles to the *Titanic* on only the third manned

Akademik Mstislav Keldysh. (Unknown Author)

expedition ever mounted to the wreck. Once on the seabed, the two subs touched down gently using a pair of skis underneath their hulls, thereby leaving less disturbance and certainly causing less of the sea bottom to be kicked up, which would have seriously reduced visibility. This gave an excellent opportunity to view the *Titanic's* propellers, only the ski tracks being left behind when they departed the scene.

The *Mir*s gently landed on the upper deck of the *Titanic* to carry out their filming. On one occasion, MacInnis landed on the bridge area but then couldn't move when it was time to leave; thankfully, the other *Mir* came to assist and found that the under-hull landing skid had become anchored under a bunch of cables on the wreck. They were able to manoeuvre the submersible forward until clear of the danger. It was a hair-raising incident that would have been so much worse if the other *Mir* had not been on hand to guide them.

Akademik Mstislav Keldysh. (Digifruitella)

After the IMAX expedition was over, the *Mir*s took part in the exploration of the submarine *I-52* and the German battleship *Bismarck*, and also carried out detailed missions to the North Pole, underneath the ice. They assisted with Russia's polar territorial claim in 2001 by placing a 1-metre-tall flagpole with the national flag into the seabed, an incident that sparked controversy worldwide but which no country actually recognises as legitimate.

When the results of the *Titanic* expedition were made public, they were shown in the IMAX documentary *Titanica*, which was a huge hit with audiences who lapped up the footage showing the wreck on the huge cinema screens. The expedition led to some incredible views of the *Titanic* that had never before been seen, with entire areas of the ship being filmed.

Scientifically, other results were being studied in labs regarding the ship itself. When one of the *Mir* submersibles brought up a piece

One of the *Mir* submersibles being hoisted from the *Keldysh* ready to dive. (NOAA)

of the *Titanic*'s steel hull, it was forensically examined using chemical analysis and a Charpy V-notch test to find its toughness in a variety of temperatures. The steel used to construct the *Titanic* was around 1½ inches thick, held together with some three million rivets made up of a combination of wrought iron and steel. The analysis concluded that the *Titanic* hull was made of brittle steel, which massively contributed to the loss of the ship. It was suggested that the cold temperatures of that fateful night in 1912, combined with the striking of the iceberg, meant that the hull simply shattered when the collision occurred. This was disputed by many academics and members of the metallurgic community, and the subject would be revisited later when further tests were carried out on a future expedition.

Among the items brought to the surface during the expedition was a collection of rusticles, the bioconcreteous structures that were first named by Robert Ballard when he noticed how they hung like icicles from the wreck. *Mir 2* deployed the manipulator arm and gently removed a number of them from the site, placing them in plastic bags in order to safely bring them to the surface without damaging them too much as they left their natural environment. They were then stored in vacuum-sealed conditions at a temperature of 4 degrees Celsius. Studies of these rusticles found a number of bacteria living within the rust, with DNA testing carried out in order to further the research into just what was living on the *Titanic* wreck and what was surviving in this unique and hostile environment.

9

MORE SALVAGE (1993-1994)

THE SUCCESS OF THE 1987 salvage expedition once again had many people talking about the *Titanic*, and despite objections to the raising of items from the wreck, it was now considered that there could be a future in salvaging further pieces for historical purposes.

The company running the salvage operations, and which now had salvage rights to the wreck, was known as RMS Titanic Inc, successor to what was previously Titanic Ventures, led by G. Michael Harris and former car salesman George Tulloch. They were determined that *Titanic* would not just sit there and rust away, but would instead reveal more about life in the Edwardian age on the most grandest of floating palaces. To do this, they enlisted the help of IFREMER.

Once again using the research vessel *Nadir* and its trusty submersible *Nautile*, the cold month of April 1993 was spent raising hundreds more artefacts, each one carefully carried back to the surface, packed in special containers where they wouldn't be allowed to dry out and crumble, then shipped to a secret location in France. Once there, conservationists worked to get them back to as near as possible their original condition. The haul included around 800 items, including a set of ship's whistles, a 2-ton engine eccentric stramp, a double lifeboat davit and even tiny items such as a child's marble.

One of those invited onto the expedition and to dive the wreck was teacher, historian and author Charles Haas, who had co-authored several books about the liner, such as *Titanic: Triumph and Tragedy* and *Titanic: Destination Disaster*, both excellent works that were popular amongst enthusiasts. Years later, he would speak about his apprehension over diving down to the wreck, with the site's 3 tons of pressure per square inch. He talked to his family about the risks involved in the dive before eventually, as he saw how professional the engineers were and the meticulous checks that were carried out before each mission, he stepped on board the *Nautile* and made the dive of a lifetime. He was enthralled by the sight of the wreck of the ship that he had written about and researched for so many years. Thoughts of anything bad happening were soon put to the back of his mind. He thus became the first ever schoolteacher to dive the *Titanic* (Haas would return to the wreck in the 1996 expedition).

Although there were many years of work ahead of them, these thousands of items relating to the *Titanic* were now being carefully cleaned and preserved, ready to be displayed in a museum or touring exhibition that would take them worldwide. But while the salvage expedition was heading back to port, a storm was brewing regarding the legal implications.

Soon after this expedition, a court case came to a head, with a rival salvage company, Marex Inc, seeking the rights to salvage items from the *Titanic*. A counter order from RMS Titanic Inc went to court to claim exclusive rights to the salvage, as they had by this time already salvaged over 2,500 items and had in effect got there first. Representatives of RMS Titanic Inc entered court with a salvaged wine decanter from the wreck in their hands. Judge J. Calvitt Clarke Jr ordered a notice of proposed action to be published in several major newspapers, which invited any party to have ownership of the *Titanic* or a better claim to the salvage to come forward. Only one other claim was made, so the US District Court for the Eastern District of Virginia awarded RMS Titanic Inc sole and exclusive ownership of any items salvaged from the *Titanic* and quashed any other attempt by any other company to be able to raise objects from in and around the wreck site. RMS Titanic Inc could now proceed as planned, with the condition that the collection be kept together and they would not sell individual items. The ruling, stamped and dated 4 June 1994, also forbade the company from cutting into the wreck and detaching any part of it.

In July 1994, the *Nadir* once again sailed from the Azores with *Nautile* to continue the work. This time, the salvage crew was eager to find for a television documentary the cause of a huge hole in the side of the ship and highlight the fire that was burning when the ship sailed from Southampton. Tulloch was convinced that the fire was 'the driving force' that caused the *Titanic* to go faster.

A Frenchman named Paul-Henri Nargeolet was in charge of the submersible. A veteran of many deep dives, he would be instrumental in making sure the dives were carried out safely and professionally. He was born in 1946 and joined the Marine Nationale (the French Navy) in 1964, specializing in underwater work and mine clearance. He left the navy in 1986 to join IFREMER, became pilot of the *Nautile* for the 1987 expedition and had been with the French *Titanic* team ever since. No stranger to shipwrecks, Nargeolet was on board *Nautile* in a dive off Toulon in 1993 when he located the wreck of the French warship *La Lune*, which had gone down in 1664.

Back on the *Titanic*, the team was already making progress with the salvage of artefacts. Syntactic foam was used to float the artefacts to the surface. Modules loaded with it were lowered to the seabed, along with specially modified baskets; items could then be carefully extracted from the seabed and gently placed in the baskets. The dives were successful, with TV cameras capturing some fascinating items being unloaded from the mud and silt – a metal door frame, a light fitting, a watch, crockery, personal items and even a jar of olives. One of the most interesting items was a pair of binoculars. This once again brought up the story of the missing pair of binoculars that could have saved the *Titanic* if the lookouts had been given them; the cupboard had been locked by Second Officer David Blair, who was then replaced by Charles Lightoller but left the ship with the key still in his pocket.

The team also wanted to find and raise some of the huge chunks of coal littering the seabed. Although they had promised they would not sell any of the items raised, they made an exception for the coal, which they planned to cut up into tiny pieces and sell as souvenirs at the *Titanic* exhibitions. There was one other thing that they wanted to bring up that would really raise the profile of the operation – a 3-ton bollard that lay in the debris field. This was a major decision, as something that big would need some careful planning and the use of floatation bags full of diesel in order to bring it to the surface (diesel being better to use than air, as air would expand as it came to the surface from 2 miles or so down and escape from the bags). Carefully hooking up the bollard to the floatation bags, the huge weight was brought to the surface and hoisted out of the water, being placed gently on the stern deck of the *Nautile*. Nargeolet and Tulloch held on to the steadying lines as the team brought the bollard to rest, the first time a major part of the *Titanic* had been seen on the surface in eighty-two years.

Further diving on the wreck involved the ROV *Robin* being deployed to look inside the wreck. Nargeolet piloted the sub gently to avoid the sharp edges of the wreckage in order to get incredible footage inside what used to be the grandest rooms afloat. The cameras were able to pick up what was left of light fittings hanging down from now-empty and rusting compartments. One of the other objectives successfully carried out on this expedition was to measure a huge 15-ton section of the hull that had broken off the ship; this was earmarked for a potential salvage operation at a later date.

Upon the return to dry land, the salvaged items were taken away once again to be worked on by conservationists. In 1996, the documentary *Explorers of the Titanic* was broadcast to a world eager to see more of the legendary wreck and what the 1994 expedition had been doing. The programme focused on Tulloch's obsession with the coal fire having contributed to the loss of the ship, despite the *Titanic* expert on board *Nadir* confirming that the coal bunker fire was extinguished by 13 April 1912, two days before the ship sank. Tulloch was convinced that the coal dust in the bunker exploded and caused the ship to sink. The lack of eyewitness testimony and examination of the wreck since then has confirmed that the damage to the side of the ship was caused by the bow section hitting the seabed and buckling the hull, the wreck of the *Titanic* having many such openings. The stern section was in such a badly damaged state that it is clear the air inside the vessel made the stern implode, plummeting to the seabed at a rate of knots. Nargeolet explained this to Tulloch, who was nevertheless adamant that the coal fire had a hand in both the damage and the sinking.

The subject of grave robbing was brought up with Tulloch but he defended his position as expedition leader, saying that the people who robbed those like Captain Stanley Lord of their reputations were grave robbers. The controversy was still there and still divides opinions to this day.

In 1991, before this expedition – and indeed the previous one – had taken place, the curators of the National Maritime Museum in Greenwich, London, had been contacted by RMS Titanic Inc, who offered them the opportunity to exhibit some of the items that had been salvaged from the wreck and had gone through the final stages of preservation, and were now able to be displayed and seen in public for the first time. Meetings were held and the proposal discussed at a high level, the potential for another organization snapping up this offer at the backs of their minds. With a chance for history to be made, the proposal was agreed and the museum began working closely with representatives of the salvage company to facilitate a new and exciting exhibition featuring items from the *Titanic*.

In October 1994, 'The Wreck of the Titanic' exhibition opened at the museum to a wave of publicity, consisting of 150 salvaged items from the wreck site, with *Titanic* survivor Millvina Dean making headlines as she looked through an original porthole from the doomed liner for the first time in eighty-two years; the last time she had done so she was just nine weeks old. It proved a very popular attraction, with more than 700,000 people seeing the artefacts on display and a high volume of media attention being generated. However, it also brought widespread criticism from around the world, from the usual emotional reactions to the exhibition of *Titanic* and disaster items to professional opinions and academics. The museum welcomed the debate, as it got people talking about the exhibition in a world long before social media took over.

This was the first of many exhibitions that would display *Titanic* artefacts around the world, telling the story of the tragedy of the sinking, the excitement of the discovery and the unique cultural history of the ship itself in film posters and survivors' stories. There were elements of bad timing too, for it was not the only shipwreck to be in the headlines as the exhibition opened. Just days before, Europe had been shocked by the sinking of the passenger ferry *Estonia* on 28 September 1994; of almost 1,000 people on board, 852 were killed in the worst peacetime shipping disaster in Europe since the Second World War. The ship had been travelling between Estonia and Sweden, the freezing Baltic Sea and huge loss of life having obvious parallels with the *Titanic* disaster. With the *Estonia* disaster fresh in people's minds, the timing of the exhibition couldn't have come at a worse moment.

10

BIG SCREEN MOVIE - THE CAMERON FILMING (1995)

THERE HAD BEEN many films about the sinking of the *Titanic*, the first one being made less than a year after the ship sank and starring one of the survivors, who played herself in the movie. One released in 1943 by the Nazi Party in Germany portrayed a heroic German officer battling against the cowardly British (which surprisingly didn't actually go down that well within the Reich). There was 1953's fictional *Titanic*, starring Barbara Stanwyck and Clifton Webb as a couple with marital issues, set against the background of the disaster, followed five years later by the classic *A Night to Remember*, based on the bestselling book of the same name. In the mid-1990s, film director James Cameron decided the story needed retelling on the big screen and in a way that had never before been done.

Cameron had a script based around the sinking *Titanic*, featuring a fictional love story that ignites between a homeless man winning a ticket on the ship and the fiancée of a rich businessman. Cameron was no stranger to making blockbusters – he had seen huge success with his *Terminator* and *Aliens* movies, and was now preparing his next one that would be made employing some of the most amazing filming techniques of his career. Not only would he use pioneering computer graphics, technology and some of the world's most well-known actors, he would use one thing that nobody else had done before – the *Titanic* itself.

Born in Canada in 1954, James Francis Cameron was working as a truck driver in his early twenties. Then he saw *Star Wars* at the cinema, which made him decide to quit his job in order to work in the film industry. He quickly learned how to direct movies, and the next few years showed that he was very good at what he did. He soon became sought-after within the industry and wrote his own scripts. One such script, *The Terminator*, was initially rejected, but he eventually managed to sell the story and was hired to direct it himself. The movie becoming hugely popular, cementing Cameron's name in the film industry.

In the early 1990s he was looking at making a big-budget movie on the story of the *Titanic*, with a production budget of an incredible $200 million, making it at the time the most expensive film ever made. Cameron set about not only making *Titanic* movie sets on dry land, but wanted to film an actual expedition out at sea and thus began to organize a series of dives on the wreck itself.

RMS Titanic Inc initially protested, as they were the salvor-in-possession of the *Titanic*. However, they took no legal action against Cameron, as he was not removing any items and was instead just visiting the wreck, so there were no legal arguments that could be made.

With a good reputation for deep-water expeditions onto seamounts, shipwrecks and the Mid-Atlantic Ridge, the *Keldysh* was hired by Cameron, using the *Mir* submersibles and having the *Titanic* itself as the star of the show. Carrying out filming over the wreck of the ship in high definition, building a huge film set on land and having the *Keldysh* as the scene-setter for the story, Cameron was on to a winner.

In September 1995, Cameron's expedition began filming the wreck of the *Titanic*, providing the production team with the best images possible in order to guide them in recreating the ship and its interior for the movie. With the dives a success, Cameron was able to concentrate on the movie script, while over the next year filming was taking place in the various locations. The team carried out twelve dives in total, each time both *Mir 1* and *Mir 2* being launched forty-five minutes apart in order to cover twice as much ground.

However, the production was not without its issues. When Cameron was interviewed years later by Radio Canada about his experiences, he recalled carrying out his third dive on the wreck when a sudden underwater 'sandstorm', whipped up by the currents, led to their submersible grounding on the seabed. His pilot, Dr Anatoly Sagalevich, turned to him and simply said 'oh no' – they both realized the serious nature of their situation. With temperatures in the submersible near freezing and the battery slowly depleting, they attempted all kinds of ways to become unstuck from the mud, but the currents were pushing them further down. It took around thirty minutes to finally release the sub from its undersea prison, and they were able to make their way back to the surface.

This was not the first time that Cameron would have issues with the dives. Later, he would talk about *Mir 1* colliding with *Titanic*'s wreckage after the new sonar on board couldn't be operated and they had to switch to an older version that the crew were more used to. The *Keldysh* also had to ride out a hurricane mid-expedition which meant a delay in the filming with the ship having to flee to a safer area around 80 miles away.

The drama soon passed and before long Cameron was back in the *Mir* sub, spending two hours slowly dropping back down to the wreck. Each time he did so, he experienced the feeling of being in a slow-moving elevator seemingly lasting a lifetime, as the temperature dropped and the pressure rose to around 6,000lb per square inch.

Cameron has described the journey in the submersibles and how the crew made sure they took a break, landing the sub gently on the wreck in order for them to have lunch. During these rest periods, with no filming taking place, they could simply stare out of the portholes and imagine what had happened to those aboard the doomed liner all those years ago. Cameron was now something of an expert on the events of 1912, and the sight of the boat deck on the bow section, with the lifeboat davit still extended, was almost overwhelming for him.

A second hurricane caused a further short delay, time that was used to review the footage already taken and show it off to members of the crew who couldn't make the dives themselves. The dramas continued with equipment failures dogging the submersibles, as well as another collision with the *Titanic* almost writing off one of the camera housings; the dive was aborted, but they then found that the power was too low to turn on the ballast pump. The slow drift back to the surface took many more hours than usual.

During another dive, *Mir 2*'s tail became entangled in one of the many cables that lay across *Titanic*'s decks, the shaking free breaking off the propeller cover and once again the dive being aborted for safety reasons.

For some of the more intricate footage and close-ups, Cameron named the ROV *Snoop Dog* (which was featured in the movie) and would send it off to explore. However, it was a frustrating time for Cameron as each sixteen-hour dive would only give about fifteen minutes of actual film footage. Nevertheless, *Snoop Dog* did manage to head along corridors inside *Titanic* and down the No 2 hatch on the bow, as well as explore the gaping hole that was once the dome above the Grand Staircase but was now just a large shaft going deep into the wreck. During one dive, the ROV was trapped for a short time as a ceiling beam collapsed, but the footage it took of the staterooms became the inspiration for the cabins that would feature in the movie. One of the set of cabins for the richest of the rich, known as the 'millionaires' suite', was occupied by a woman called Charlotte Cardeza and her son, Thomas, who had cabins B-51, B-53 and B-55. In the movie, the fictional family are housed in cabins B-52, B-54 and B-56, which were actually the ones occupied by White Star Line chairman J. Bruce Ismay. Cameron wanted to go as far as possible with the ROV, and in doing so looked at areas of the ship that had not been seen by human eyes in eighty-three years. The enormity of what he was seeing was not lost on him as he looked through the camera's eye and wondered just what went on here during those four days that *Titanic* was at sea.

The *Keldysh* spent a total of twenty-five days at sea and achieved an immense amount of research for Cameron and his team. The footage was sent to his digital laboratory, where it was used as a reference for models, backgrounds and reproducing scenes throughout the film.

Cameron's plot for the movie was a fictional love story surrounded by factual events. The people around the ship were all based on real people, but interacted with the main fictional characters. The focus is on Jack, a homeless man who wins a ticket on board *Titanic* after a card game, and Rose, a woman who is about to marry her rich fiancé and inherit a fortune. Jack and Rose meet one night and fall in love; it is one of the most talked about love stories in modern movie history. This is all set against the background of the four-day voyage from Southampton, and ending with the ship hitting the iceberg and the subsequent fight for survival. The movie had a cast of both new faces and up-and-coming stars. Kate Winslet and Leonardo DiCaprio took the main roles as the young lovers, but two longer-established actors were veterans of previous *Titanic* movies. David Warner played the valet Spicer Lovejoy in Cameron's film and passenger Lawrence Beesley in the 1979 TV movie *SOS Titanic*, while Bernard Fox now portrayed Colonel Archibald Gracie, a first-class passenger, but was also lookout Fred Fleet in the 1958 classic *A Night to Remember*.

Cameron's *Titanic* was released in late 1997 (early 1998 in the UK) and smashed all box office records, while gaining an incredible eleven Academy Awards on Oscars night. At the time, it was not only the most expensive film ever made but the highest-grossing, and it still jointly holds the record for the number of Oscars with *Ben Hur* (1959).

Contrary to popular belief, the footage used in the dives was not eventually used in the movie. Models were used to mock up what they had seen, but the submersible and the research ship were all real.

The numerous incidents of bangs and scrapes with the wreck of the *Titanic* left a lot of people with a bad feeling towards Cameron's expedition, notably regarding the pieces of the *Mir* that came off as well as a number of areas that had been damaged on the wreck during the collisions. As salvor in possession, RMS Titanic Inc could have kicked off about this. However, it should be kept in mind that the same company used the *Keldysh* and *Mir* submersibles for their own dives, so perhaps not raising too much hell over the damage to the wreck was a wise decision, given that there were few other submersibles that could go down that deep. Although all the damage was accidental and certainly not malicious, in just twelve days of diving the wreck had suffered more damage from submersible collisions than it had from the natural decaying of the hull over several years.

But this was not the end of James Cameron's association with the world's most famous liner. He was now connected to *Titanic* in more ways than one, not least that his name was linked to the most successful movie of all time. From a young age, he had always been a bit of an explorer; now he wanted to go further, promising that these dives to the *Titanic* would not be his last.

11

RAISING 'THE BIG PIECE' - PART 1 (1996)

THE POPULARITY OF ANYTHING relating to the *Titanic* reached its pinnacle after the wreck expeditions of 1987, 1993 and 1994, and the idea was now discussed of raising something a little bit larger than anything that had been done before. Tulloch and his team wanted to salvage a huge 15-ton section of the vessel which had been photographed in the debris field, and a plan was hatched to attempt to raise this chunk of hull in order to preserve it and place it on display along with the other artefacts. Surveys had already found that the rusting piece of metal – nicknamed 'The Big Piece' – was around 12ft by 26ft in size, and had originally been located between the third and fourth funnels. A new expedition would require a research ship and two support ships to ensure The Big Piece could be raised without it being damaged in the process, as well as two cruise liners, the *Royal Majesty* and *Island Breeze*, full of passengers moored nearby to watch the raising of the historic artefact.

For *Titanic* author and historian David Hutchings, this was a remarkable opportunity to see a part of the story of the *Titanic* in front of his own eyes. At the same time, he could share his knowledge of the great ship, for he had been personally invited aboard the *Royal Majesty* to be guest lecturer as events were organized that would allow passengers on board to be part of the *Titanic*-themed educational and historical

Raising The Big Piece expedition in 1996, showing *Ocean Voyager* and *Nadir*. (David Hutchings)

journey. On board this ship would be 86-year-old Eleanor Johnson Schumann from Illinois, who survived the sinking as an 18-month-old child, while on the *Island Breeze* would be another survivor, 99-year-old Edith Haisman from the UK, as well as several other prominent historians and experts related to the *Titanic* story. Hutchings boarded a plane for Boston, Massachusetts, and on 25 August 1996 stepped onto the *Royal Majesty*. With so much publicity surrounding the expedition, he was interviewed by two different newspapers on the quayside before he had even got on board.

The liner sailed that afternoon, heading out to the site of the *Titanic* wreck. Hutchings gave his first lecture the following morning to a crowded lounge, in what he later said he thought would be a ship packed with *Titanic* experts but instead turned out to be full of people eager to learn. He was constantly stopped to be asked questions about the ship, which he was only too pleased to answer.

Two days later, the liner neared the wreckage site, the *Island Breeze* already on station with the recovery and survey ships. The White Star flag was hoisted up the flagpole of the *Royal Majesty* and brought down to half-mast to signify that they were now at the site of the *Titanic* disaster. The other ships were now all together; *Nadir* with *Nautile* would conduct the dives, the *Ocean Voyager* giving support to the dive teams with matters such as lighting, and there was the recovery ship *Jim Kilabuk* that would lift The Big Piece when the time came. The *Jim Kilabuk* was a 207ft-long Canadian offshore supply ship that was built in 1975 at the Versatile Pacific Victoria shipyard in Esquimalt on Vancouver Island. Launched as the *Canmar Supplier IV*, it was renamed *Holly B* in 1994 then very quickly became the *Pernell J* before finally becoming *Jim Kilabuk* in June 1995. At 1,261 gross tons, its structure was the perfect set-up for a major recovery operation of this magnitude, with a wide, open-spaced deck aft, a forward superstructure and a heavy-duty A-frame aft for The Big Piece to be set down on the stern and lashed down for the journey back to dry land.

For the next two days, the salvage team worked hard to rig up The Big Piece for the final lift, the two liners circling with anticipation as the events on board told the story of the *Titanic* for guests and highlighted what had happened here eighty-four years previously. Live coverage of what was happening on board *Nadir* and the wreck site was shown

The liner *Island Breeze* with support ship *Jim Kilabuk*, showing the lifting bags astern. (David Hutchings)

On the *Royal Majesty*, the White Star pennant is flown at half-mast as they reach the wreck site. (David Hutchings)

in the cabin televisions, and large screens were set up in the theatres and lounges as the events continued to educate and inspire those who had come to learn about the history of the *Titanic*. Numerous movies were shown in the theatres, where guests could watch the likes of *SOS Titanic* and *A Night to Remember* to get a feel for the drama that had played out at the exact place where they now were.

In between lectures, Hutchings was rubbing shoulders with a variety of interesting people, such as the great-granddaughter of Charles Lightoller (*Titanic*'s Second Officer and senior surviving crew member), the grandson of lost passenger Benjamin Guggenheim and an appearance by astronaut Buzz Aldren, the second person to walk on the Moon. Aldren had just dived the wreck and was happy to show Hutchings the images he had taken from his time on board the *Nautile* the previous day.

During the night, the liners would host a display of experiments to show audiences some of the aspects of the story that had been

Jim Kilabuk taking station, preparing to lift The Big Piece in 1996. (David Hutchings)

challenged in the past as well as being points of discussion for many decades. The original plans for the *Titanic*'s rockets had been used to make replicas which were fired off as the '*Californian* Incident' was re-enacted to show what it was really like that night. The *Jim Kilabuk* was placed in position 8 miles away from the liners and the *Ocean Voyager* was sent 19 miles away, the two positions that had been hotly disputed at the time. The 1912 inquiry stated that the Leyland Liner *Californian* had been close to the *Titanic* and therefore should have seen the distressed ship, but Captain Stanley Lord had insisted that he was around 19 miles away and stuck in ice. The two support ships took it in turns to fire their rockets as Hutchings gave a commentary. None of the rockets were actually heard, but they were clearly seen. Next he gave the Captain of the *Royal Majesty* instructions as to where to position his ship and then extinguish the lights, showing that it would be impossible to confuse a fully lit vessel at night with one that just had mast-head lights showing. In the early hours of the morning, the experiment was

Nadir above the wreck. (David Hutchings)

Nadir above the wreck. (David Hutchings)

completed and the interest sparked that night once again became a talking point on board.

On Wednesday 28 August, it was time for the lifting to take place. The huge section of *Titanic*'s hull had by now been rigged up to lifting bags full of diesel fuel, which had been lowered to the seabed by the use of huge chains weighing them down, a remote control switch allowing them to fall away and hopefully float The Big Piece to the surface. Unfortunately, there was a problem activating half of the transducers and the hull section was now suspended vertically, half off the seabed. The next twenty-four hours were spent trying to release the two chains, but a further complication led to *Nautile* taking another bag of diesel down after one of them was accidentally cut and suddenly rushed to the surface. When the time came and the go-ahead was given, the announcement was made on the liners that The Big Piece was finally on its way up. Crowds rushed onto the upper decks of the surrounding ships as the lifting bags broke the surface, cheers rang out to congratulate the people working hard to

A sea-boat from *Ocean Voyager* at the lifting bags on the surface, preparing to raise the *Titanic* wreckage. (David Hutchings)

achieve all this, but a later press report of a 'carnival atmosphere' simply didn't happen, as those on board knew the significance of this event.

Further problems then arose when one of the lifting bags suddenly exploded and diesel was floating on the sea's surface. Meanwhile, the cables underwater were becoming tangled, the divers unable to do anything to help as it was too deep still for them to deploy.

As the divers and engineers worked into the night, a memorial ceremony was held on the two liners, a list of names being read out of those who had perished in 1912. The length of time it took to read out all the names visibly shocked those who were present, each name representing a human life lost.

The next day, the *Island Breeze* and *Royal Majesty* had to depart the wreck site, with The Big Piece still suspended 300ft below the surface as the *Jim Kilabuk* tried to move into position for the recovery phase. With the sea state getting worse, an attempt to tow the section to shallower waters proved too much for the strain on the cables and

Memorial ceremony on the *Royal Majesty* above the wreck site. (David Hutchings)

P.H. Nargeolet and George Tulloch talk to the people involved in the 1996 expedition, assuring them that they would be back soon to continue the mission. (David Hutchings)

David Hutchings back on dry land after spending the previous week giving lectures on the *Titanic* for the guests on the *Royal Majesty*. (David Hutchings)

they parted, sending it back to the seabed. By coincidence, it went back down to the ocean floor just before 0220hrs, the exact time of night that the *Titanic* had originally sunk. The position of The Big Piece was noted, and while headlines later told of the disappointment of some of those on board the two liners at the failure to recover The Big Piece, the salvage teams were undeterred and soon announced that they would return to recover the wreckage at a later date.

On Sunday 1 September, the *Royal Majesty* docked in Boston and David Hutchings disembarked for a reception laid on for those who had been part of the expedition as well as the *Titanic* survivors. They were joined by George Tulloch, the expedition leader, and *Nautile* pilot Paul-Henri Nargeolet, who spoke after being rushed back from the wreck site in order to meet everybody. With Hurricane Edward about to cause damage to the eastern seaboard of the United States, the expedition was suspended and Hutchings flew back home to the UK.

Titanic survivor Edith Haisman realized two ambitions this year. She had wanted to visit the site where her father died and live to be 100 years old. She achieved both of these, passing away peacefully just a few months later in January 1997.

12

RAISING 'THE BIG PIECE' - PART 2 (1998)

TWO YEARS SINCE the salvage operation had been dramatically cut short, the offshore supply vessel *Abeille Supporter* became the ship of choice for the next attempt to raise the elusive chunk of *Titanic*. Built in Vard Aukra, Norway, in 1975 as the *Seaway Hawk*, it had been renamed *Abeille Supporter* (IMO Number 7382433) in 1982 for the French Ministry of Defence. At 208ft long and weighing 1,323 gross tons, the heavy-duty tug normally catered for rigs in the oil industry, but now this yellow-hulled vessel had been hired for the *Titanic* expedition to conduct their most audacious salvage operation yet. It was to attempt to hoist the fragile piece of the liner as well as keep it steady while transporting it back to shore.

With it was the 191ft-long research vessel *Ocean Voyager* from the previous expedition. At 1,540 gross tons, this ship was launched in 1974 as the *Pandora II*, being renamed *Jean Francoise de la Pe* in 1994 but only lasting a year under that name before becoming *Ocean Voyager*, all the while still being owned by the same company. Resembling a cross between a luxury yacht and a tourist vessel, *Ocean Voyager*'s white hull sported two small funnels in the midships section behind the bridge, a large dome for communications and a large blue A-frame at the stern for launch and recovery of underwater vehicles. It had been built at the Bel Aire Shipyard, Vancouver, Canada, and

Ocean Voyager at Blyth in 1997 in between *Titanic* expeditions. (Henry Pattison)

was owned by the Northlake Shipping Ltd, Canada (IMO number 7343645).

Fitted out for survey work, *Ocean Voyager* had the words 'Titanic 98' just under the bridge screen, advertising the ship's mission as it left port that summer of 1998. It was filled with eager people who hoped to see a real-life version of *Raise the Titanic* right in front of their eyes, although the disappointment of events two years before was still on their minds. Using careful techniques and again the lifting bags full of fuel, it was hoped that the massive piece of the wreck of the *Titanic* would finally break the surface, to the delight of the teams who had spent so long preparing for this moment.

Now laying on the seabed far away from its original location near the wreck, The Big Piece was hooked up once again to the lifting bags. Soon afterwards, the massive chunk of metal – the largest part of the liner to be attempted to be raised – which contained a number of portholes and the *Titanic*'s famous signature rivets, slowly

Christos XXIII (formerly the *Abeille Supporter*) towing HMS *Ark Royal* for scrap in Portsmouth, 20 May 2013. (Author)

made its way to the surface. In full view of all those on the support ships, it broke the surface and was finally hoisted on board *Abeille Supporter* after two years of hard work and frustrating setbacks. The culmination of the complex operation created memorable images for television documentaries as cameras captured every second of the recovery.

Once it was gently laid on the deck of the ship, The Big Piece was taken straight to Boston, Massachusetts, where it underwent metallurgical and structural analysis. The design of the riveted joints was later found to be a contributing factor in the flooding of the ship, the ice having simply popped the rivets. While the preservation team carried out this work, the rest of the expedition continued with further planned dives to the *Titanic*. It was not just The Big Piece that would make the 1998 expedition worthwhile, as the ROV *Magellan* was deployed to explore different parts of the wreck and conduct scientific tests in an attempt to answer questions that had been asked ever since the *Titanic* had been found.

During one of the dives, a single sediment sample was taken from the seafloor close to the stern section of the wreck. Although they could not manage to get a proper sample using a core barrel from either *Magellan* or the *Nautile*, they did get *Nautile* to dig down with a shovel-type implement that allowed a sample around 20–30cm in depth. Analysis of this sample showed that a previous theory of the bow hitting the seabed at a steep angle and high speed was actually wrong. Instead, hydronamic investigation found that the most likely scenario was that the *Titanic* went down at around 5–10 metres per second and at a shallow angle of no more than 40 degrees. Previous tests had only been carried out on a model in a lab on shore. Notwithstanding this new theory, the bow was buried up to the anchors, with an average depth of around 12 metres. With scientific analysis of the sample and the composition of the seabed

Christos XXIII with *Ark Royal*, Portsmouth, 17 May 2013. (Author)

now being known up to a point, the information gained was invaluable. Scientists could determine the velocity and angle of impact of the wreck, but they also had to know the strength of the seafloor and sub-bottom sediments. Now this had been achieved, it opened up a new avenue of investigation for this part of the *Titanic* story.

This had been the second investigation in a row where investigations were carried out to analyse the theory of the *Titanic* having a brittle fracture. RMS Titanic Inc and the Discovery Channel used these two visits of 1996 and 1998 to conduct a forensic analysis of the wreckage, using the expertise of the Marine Forensics Panel of the Society of Naval Architects and Marine Engineers. The equipment used was a sub-bottom profiler and side-scan sonar, and the ship was surveyed along the starboard side to determine just how much damage was caused when the *Titanic* had hit the iceberg. The low frequency acoustic returns were aimed towards the general area of

Christos XXIII with *Ark Royal*, Portsmouth, 16 May 2013. (Author)

the hull section in question and also penetrated the seabed to provide an image of what the damage below the mud looked like after over eighty years.

The results from this scan showed that only around 12 square feet of the hull of the *Titanic* was damaged by impact with the iceberg, completely debunking previous theories of a 300ft gash. The hole that actually sank the *Titanic* comprised six narrow openings caused by the ice running from the forepeak tank to Boiler Room Number 6, ranging from small slits to much larger breaks in the riveted hull. In effect, the ice had popped the staples that were holding the *Titanic* together.

Around three million rivets were used to build *Titanic* in Belfast. Samples of the hull itself found that the steel was actually not brittle as first suspected; instead, it was the rivets popping in the collision with the ice that had caused the ship's hull to open up to the sea so easily. The brittle steel theory was disproved beyond doubt when a piece of the hull was subjected to a number of tests involving a slow-bend, being struck with a pendulum hammer and other analysis, all of which put to bed the initial conclusions that were reached after the 1991 expedition.

The tests also highlighted the fact that the quality of the steel on the *Titanic* was actually very good, with the manufacturing described as state-of-the-art for the steel of that era. Indeed, it had some 80 per cent of the toughness of similar steel found today. It was the rivets themselves that were not of high quality. However, it was said that Harland and Wolff were not to blame for this and the subsequent loss of the ship, as back in 1911 there was no quality control for monitoring such building methods or materials. The problem was nothing to do with how the rivets were fitted to the ship; it was the rivets themselves which were the issue.

This was all put together in a number of fascinating new documentaries for the Discovery Channel, including *Titanic: Anatomy of a Disaster*. They also examined how the stresses of the

Christos XXIII with *Ark Royal*, Portsmouth, 16 May 2013. (Author)

open spaces on board the ship led to the *Titanic* breaking in two as the stern lifted high into the air. The wide open areas of the public rooms caused stresses and bends to form, and eventually the sheer weight of the aft section of the liner was simply too much and the hull was ripped in half by its own tonnage.

This is not to say that the steel was a massive failure, but any ship with that amount of stress placed upon it, without anything to hold it up, would be left at a point of no return.

In the meantime, work was being carried out on The Big Piece. Preservation work and strengthening were progressing well, although due to issues about its size and the ability to store, preserve and transport it, the hull section was cut into two sections, the bottom half then earning the nickname 'The Little Piece'. Once the work had been completed on the two sections, they were placed on display with the other hundreds of artefacts as one of the star exhibits, an actual part of *Titanic* that could be touched and seen by millions of visitors all year round in the ever-popular exhibitions. The centrepieces of the displays were a door from D-Deck and The Big Piece, crowds turning up in their masses to see these pieces of *Titanic* that had by now featured in countless TV news reports and dozens of documentaries.

The 1998 expedition was a huge success. The salvage had gone to plan and investigations had uncovered new evidence about the demise of the *Titanic*. As for the expedition ships, the *Abeille Supporter* was sold and renamed in 2000 as the *Aquitaine Explorer*, then *Greek Explorer* in June 2010 and by the end of that year becoming *Christos XXIII*. In May 2013, it was chosen to tow the old aircraft carrier HMS *Ark Royal* from Portsmouth naval base in the UK to its final destination at a Turkish scrapyard, a journey of several thousand miles through the Bay of Biscay and across the Mediterranean.

In November 2022, *Christos XXIII* was sold for scrapping at Aliaga in Turkey, where it arrived for breaking up the following month. The ship had forty years of experience, its most famous role having nothing to do with its original design specification.

The *Ocean Voyager* met with disaster just four years after the Big Piece expedition. Under charter to survey company Gardline, the *Ocean Voyager* was tasked to conduct a survey of the seabed off the coast of Oman in the summer of 2002. On 9 July, accompanied by support vessel *Miclyn Searcher*, it sailed to a position around

135 miles from the coast to meet up with a third survey vessel, the *Ocean Endeavour*. They were to carry out surveys for a proposed gas pipeline between Iran, India and Oman. For the twenty-nine crew members on board *Ocean Voyager*, the first part of the survey involved setting up the equipment.

By the following day, 10 July, the ships were on site. An acoustic transceiver pole was deployed through a hole in the ship's hull through the engine room via a gland, support stool and gate valve. As the 5-metre-long pole was gently lowered using a chain block assembly, the pole suddenly fell some 4–5 metres. Weighing around 500kg, the pole caused damage to a retaining collar and some of the supporting structures, and water started to flood into the ship.

The ship quickly arranged a rescue operation, but before long it was realized that although the *Ocean Voyager* was sinking, there was no real danger to life. Three pumps were taken on board via helicopter from various United States warships in the area, although frustratingly, only one of the pumps actually worked. Gardline emergency response teams made contact with various support services in Oman and Iran as the fight to save the ship continued.

Nevertheless, the fight proved in vain as the incoming water overwhelmed the efforts of the crew. Before long, the fight to save the ship was abandoned, with all her crew transferred to the nearby *Miclyn Searcher*, from where they watched their ship be slowly consumed by the waves. For the next three hours, the ships stood by as the *Ocean Voyager* continued its sharp list to starboard. It then slowly slipped under, going down by the bow and having the stern pointing skywards before disappearing beneath the warm waters of the Gulf of Oman, sinking some 3km to the seabed.

Meanwhile, on the other side of the world, another company entered the *Titanic* story. The UK-based Deep Ocean Expeditions offered tourists the opportunity to visit the wreck using the *Mir* submersibles for around $32,500 per person, with forty-five people instantly making inquiries. However, back in court, Judge Clarke

Rob McCallum, the head of Deep Ocean Exploration, who began his *Titanic* expeditions in 1998. (Rob McCallum)

proceeded to ban anyone in the world from entering a 168 square mile exclusion zone around the wreck in favour of RMS Titanic Inc, stopping even innocent visits to the wreck, in effect taking control of territory well outside the borders of the United States. Deep Ocean Expeditions (DOE), led by Robert McCallum, lodged an appeal with the US Court of Appeals in Richmond, Virginia. The decision was later overturned, with DOE permitted to go ahead with their planned dives, which commenced in September 1998. McCallum and DOE thereafter became the place to go for those wanting to book trips to the *Titanic*, for whatever reason.

Born in New Zealand, McCallum wanted to access the most inhospitable places on Earth and to make these deep ocean areas accessible to anyone able to afford the immense costs that would come with launching an expedition to places such as the wreck of the *Titanic*. This first *Titanic* expedition would be the first of several high-profile visits to the wreck over the years.

Setting sail on the *Keldysh*, McCallum headed out to sea with his first '*Titanic* tourists', and dives took place from 9–13 September 1998 using both *Mir* submersibles. Four dives were conducted over each of those five days, each one carrying two passengers. The initial success of the company organizing these dives cemented its ability to visit the wreck, allowing a single point of contact for those needing to film *Titanic* for a new documentary, wishing to carry out scientific analysis or simply wanting to visit the most famous shipwreck in the world.

The results of these DOE trips have remained something of a mystery, with no public declaration of what went on and who made the dives. All that is known for certain is that the *Keldysh* and the *Mir* submersibles were used for the expeditions.

With the controversy over deep-sea tourism to the *Titanic* rearing its head, many questioned the ethical implications of people going down to a disaster site like it was some kind of funfair ride. The argument between the preserving of history and presenting a spectacle is one that continues to this day.

13

THE LATE 1990s AND THE WRECK OF THE *BRITANNIC*

ROBERT MCCALLUM and Deep Ocean Exploration returned to the wreck of the *Titanic* in September 1999. The *Keldysh* sailed from St John's in Newfoundland and arrived at the site a few days later on 14 September, launching the two *Mir* submersibles to allow four people at a time, along with the two pilots, to head down to the wreck for their visits. The double dives went on for five days before the *Keldysh* returned to port, having carried twenty people to the depths.

One of those was Paul Boyle, who was interviewed soon after by the *Donegal News* as he was thought to be the first Irish visitor to the *Titanic* wreck. Boyle had entered a radio competition for a trip to see the wreck of the *Titanic*, and was thrilled to find that he had won the prize of a lifetime. He was allowed to familiarize himself with the *Mir* submersibles by spending time inside one of them with the hatch closed, in order to ensure he had no issues with confined spaces.

Two days after the *Keldysh* appeared on site, the crew had gathered at 0900hrs to launch the submersibles. Boyle was escorted through the hatch for his twelve-hour trip to the seabed. One thing he particularly remembered was when the submersible struck part of the *Titanic*, the vessel resting on the deck of the wreck while everybody on board ate their lunch.

Boyle added that before long the dive was over, the ascent back to the surface taking two or three hours, after which the jump crew hooked up the *Mir* and the submersible was hoisted back on board. The engineers then carried out their post-dive maintenance routine as the submersible passengers left via the hatch with memories that would stay with them for life.

It was the collision with the wreck that stuck with Boyle, especially seeing the look of concern in the eyes of the pilot. It was on this expedition that scientists recorded the state of the wreck to assess the level of deterioration; the plan was to revisit the wreck in years to come to see how time and travellers had left their mark on it.

With the *Mir* submersibles setting down on the wreck every time they descended to stop for a break, these slight collisions would over time speed up the gradual collapse of the wreck. Experts estimated that in around forty years there would be nothing left of the *Titanic*. Later expeditions would show just how significant these trips and collisions with the wreck would be.

This year was also significant for Caroline Graham, the Los Angeles Editor of British newspaper *The Mail on Sunday*, who had started her career in journalism back home in Surrey for a local newspaper before going to *The Sun* in 1989. By 1992 she had moved to California in her capacity as a *Sun* reporter, and had gone on to join *The Mail on Sunday* by 1999. She had met *National Geographic* photographer Ralph White, who had been part of the original team that found the *Titanic* wreck and had since been back to the site on a number of occasions. Graham decided to do a story on his fascinating adventures. White highlighted to her that tourists could now pay to dive the wreck of the *Titanic*, and when Graham got in touch with Mike McDowell, the owner of DOE and heavily involved in the expeditions, he invited her newspaper to come along and write about the trip. After chatting with her editor, Peter Wright, the go-ahead was given and she soon found herself on the deck of the *Keldysh*, interviewing those on board the *Titanic* expedition – staff, crew members and fee-paying passengers – to cover the story of the expedition in what she hoped was going to be a great article. The Russian crew seemed to be working round the clock preparing the submersibles and getting stuck into the scientific work continually taking place on board. Everyone seemed to be working really hard and constantly having things to do, which she found fascinating to watch.

Caroline Graham then climbed aboard *Mir 1* ready for a descent to a place that still very few people had experienced. She wrote to the author in 2024 describing her first dive to *Titanic*:

> 'It's one of the most remarkable trips I have ever had the privilege to take part in. I wasn't really sure what to expect. Huge excitement beforehand. Then once the hatch closes and you start to descend the "real" world disappears very quickly. I can only describe it as calm and womblike. No fear at all. Just peace. Anatoly Sagalevich was piloting *Mir 1* and he would turn on the lights periodically on the way down. It was incredible – and unexpected – to me that there was life in some form all the way down, including at the bottom of the ocean. I saw the iridescent layer which was like the best light show ever – weird creatures, some which looked like shrimp, others like strings of pearls – all colourless. As the light shone on them they lit up. And lots of flat fish and jelly fish. I think the amount of life took me aback. I'd imagined it would be cold and dead at those depths. In fact, the ocean is teeming with life. It makes we wonder what is down there that we don't know about yet?'

As *Mir 1* landed on the seabed and then slowly came back up again, the sight of the bow of the *Titanic* took her breath away. Portholes still had glass in them, and it was at this point that the enormity of the disaster hit home, the thoughts of the last people to ever stare out of that glass running through her mind: 'I think what has stayed with me is the feeling of overwhelming sadness when you see things like two leather shoes, embedded in the ocean floor, clearly where a body fell. And the minutia of life – stacks of plates, wine bottles, a children's toy, a chair – all sitting there in the cold depths.'

Mir 1 was set down on the wreck and Graham sat having sandwiches and drinking tea out of a flask as the team rested. The submersible hovered slowly over the wreck site and gave her the experience of a lifetime. Ironically, she had never previously had much of an interest in the *Titanic*, but she felt very privileged to be in a position in a working capacity on a dive that so many people would have given their right arm for.

After twelve hours cramped up in the small sphere, the dive was over and *Mir 1* was brought back to the surface and on board *Keldysh*, with champagne given to the crew for a successful dive. A tradition for any of the dives is to fix a mesh bag of polystyrene cups to the outside of the submersible, as when it returns to the surface the pressure of the water is clear to see as they shrink down to a miniature version, a souvenir for anybody who wants to show off the power of the ocean depths!

Just four days after stepping out of *Mir 1*, her article was ready, and on 19 September 1999 *The Mail on Sunday* published Graham's three-part special called 'My Dive to *Titanic*'.

It was around this time that another part of the *Titanic* story started to become significant – the liner's sister ship, *Britannic*. A number of recent expeditions had taken place highlighting the wreck of the *Britannic* laid on the seabed off the coast of the Greek island of Kea in the Aegean.

On 21 November 1916, the *Britannic* was heading through the Kea Channel in its role as a hospital ship to take some of the wounded from the First World War in Eastern Europe. It was a journey that the

The wreck of the *Britannic*. (Stuart Williamson)

ship had made five times already, each time successfully bringing wounded military personnel back to the United Kingdom, where they could be treated in hospitals on the south coast, with the *Britannic* sent back to the Mediterranean.

This was not a role that was without danger, as there had been numerous submarine attacks on hospital ships, notably the *Asturias*, which had been targeted by a submarine but the torpedo had failed to detonate.

The crew of *Britannic* was unaware that a German submarine had laid mines in the Kea Channel, and as the ship transited through the passage that morning a huge explosion shook the liner. It took only fifty-five minutes for the liner – which was around the same size as *Titanic* – to sink, but in that time all 1,066 people on board – hospital staff, nurses and crew – were successfully evacuated. Mercifully, the ship was not on its return journey loaded with patients, as the death toll would have been horrific.

As Captain Bartlett tried to run the ship aground to save it, *Britannic* sank lower and its propellers, still turning, started to be raised out of the water. Tragedy then struck, as a lifeboat was sucked into the rotating blades of one of the propellers and hacked to pieces in front of horrified survivors in the other boats. Thirty people were killed.

Britannic settled on the seabed on its starboard side, the bow broken and bent inwards where it had struck the bottom of the Kea Channel, but otherwise the wreck was fairly intact. In an amazing coincidence, there were several *Titanic* survivors on board; this was the second time that people such as Violet Jessop and Arthur John Priest had survived the sinking of a White Star liner. In Priest's case, he had also survived *Olympic*'s collision with HMS *Hawke* as well as the loss of the *Alcantara* earlier that year, and would be one of those pulled alive from the wreck of the *Donegal* just months later.

There were no dives to survey the sunken *Britannic* until it was discovered by French ocean explorer Jacques Cousteau in 1975 and explored the following year for a documentary that questioned whether the sinking was caused by a mine or torpedo.

Twenty years later, along came Robert Ballard, who had made his name by discovering the *Titanic* and *Bismarck*. He had been at the forefront of ocean exploration for thirty years. He now wanted people to leave the *Titanic* wreck alone and instead explore the more accessible *Britannic*, turning it into an underwater museum where safer exploration could take place without damaging the wreck or the huge expense or risk to life from submersible expeditions.

Ballard found that the original survey by Cousteau had mentioned a huge hole in the port side of the ship, evidence of a possible torpedo strike or even an internal explosion. But what Ballard now found was the huge crack where the bow had disconnected from the rest of the ship. With technological advances, a better survey could be carried out using ROVs and even the nuclear mini-submarine *NR-1*, the only one of its kind in the world.

A year later, British film-maker Simon Mills bought the wreck from the British Government, owned by them as *Britannic* had been operating under the Crown at the time of loss. Nonetheless, he would still need permission to dive the wreck as it was in Greek waters. Since his purchase, Mills has given permission for a number of diving expeditions to take place. The wreck, sitting around 400ft deep, has thereby been the subject of investigations and documentary filming, with many hours of fresh footage uncovering new information about the loss of this iconic ship.

Britannic had been launched just before the start of the First World War, and by the time it was fitted out the ship was already being painted white and requisitioned as HMHS rather than RMS *Britannic*. *Titanic* was on its first (and only) voyage for four days, and it spent only a week in Southampton, but in that time many photographs were taken revealing the magnificence of the liner. But as the *Britannic* was immediately converted into a hospital ship, it was never fitted out for passenger service – and wasn't due to be until the war was over; only then would *Britannic* have been made into the luxurious and opulent liner that it was designed to be.

So despite its many months of service, very few photographs were ever taken inside the ship. Few people cared what the wards looked like on a hospital ship, and there was nothing really of interest to photograph in this very clinical and business-like vessel.

That is why it is important to penetrate this shipwreck while it is still structurally sound and able to be visited by divers with the right equipment. Expeditions from 1997 onwards have led to a small but important number of internal images, giving a unique insight into the story of this hospital ship.

A number of technical diving experts made some well-organized expeditions that appeared in diving magazines worldwide and featured in TV documentaries, highlighting that the forgotten sister to *Titanic* was forgotten no more. Although there continue to be many diplomatic issues and bureaucratic problems that seem to arise with the local authorities, when dives do take place they provide a wealth of information on the story of the *Britannic*.

A number of these expeditions, including Ballard's 1995 trip, attempted to find evidence of a minefield. Over time, there has been some success in doing so, although most of what is known about this now has come from the archives rather than the dives. Near to the wreck site is another liner that fell victim to the same minefield – that of the *Burdigala*, which had gone down a week before the loss of the *Britannic*.

Expeditions are not without tragedy, and 39-year-old Carl Spencer became the first diver to die on the wreck of *Britannic*. Part of a documentary dive crew for National Geographic, he had worked on a number of shipwrecks over many years and had visited the *Titanic* in 2003. In May 2009, during a decompression stop, Spencer had a seizure and lost consciousness, all attempts to revive him proving unsuccessful.

The huge hulk that lies off the island of Kea is still being dived. Ironically, despite it being more accessible technically, there have actually been fewer people visit *Britannic* than *Titanic*, and not as many dives as its more famous sister ship. For now, the lure of the *Britannic* continues to attract attention, but there is no sign of *Titanic* being left alone in favour of its less-glamorous sibling.

14

SALVAGE (2000)

FOR THE SIXTH expedition by RMS Titanic Inc, the company hired the Russian Academy of Science to carry out their next mission. In 2000, they gathered their equipment together and sailed back to the wreck site on board the *Akademik Mstislav Keldysh* and its *Mir* submersibles, which were being tasked to carry out the next round of artefact recovery. The expedition leaders had a plan of action of what they wanted to recover from the wreck site, and this included the navigation bridge steering stand, main wheel and steering stand, capstan controller wheel and a variety of other steering and navigational items.

The first *Titanic* wreck dive of the twenty-first century was carried out on 29 July 2000, with David Concannon climbing on board *Mir 1* ready to take the plunge. His company, Explorer Consulting, organizes these trips for those wanting to go down to the *Titanic* wreck. He was heading down to the wreck following a bumpy journey to the site, 30ft waves battering the *Keldysh*, with a 45-knot wind thrown into the equation; this went on for a number of days. Now the weather had calmed, Concannon was suitably squashed into the tiny sphere along with pilot Anatoly Sagalevich and *National Geographic* cinematographer Ralph White, both veterans of *Titanic* expeditions.

The submersible was launched, and the hot temperatures on the surface soon became more comfortable, but they knew that it would get much colder in the slow descent, which would be the point that the

David Concannon on board the *Mir 2* during the 2001 expedition. (David Concannon)

crew would start to layer up with more clothing. Around them were the dials, switches, lights and instruments that made this contraption a technological marvel. A red button in a steel cage catches Concannon's eye – only to be pressed in an absolute emergency if both of the other two on board were incapacitated. Hitting this would release the ballast and send an emergency signal to the surface vessel, alerting them that the sub was heading to the surface. Hopefully this would never be used.

It was almost midday when *Mir 1* reached the seafloor, around half a mile from the wreck of the *Titanic*. The submersible slowly made its way using sonar and a compass, sea creatures passing the view ports like something from an alien world. The noise of the control team on board the *Keldysh* broke in every so often, in Russian of course. Half an hour after reaching the seabed, the huge wreck of the *Titanic* emerged from the darkness, buried up to its anchors.

Waiting a moment for *Mir 2* to join them, Concannon was captivated by the sight of the port side of the *Titanic* rusting away, looking 'like it is made of wet sand' with the rusticles dripping down the side of the ship. This sight was not the one he was expecting, despite knowing what the ship now looked like after many days leading up to the dive spent studying the wreck. The submersibles slowly moved over the bow, the spare anchor, the mast, bridge, each area captivating all three in *Mir 1*.

One thing he found particularly fascinating was when the submersible was set down on top of the deck, and he looked out of the view port to see his own reflection in a piece of glass on the wreck. It was a surreal moment seeing his own face staring back at him from the *Titanic*. A call from the surface announced that the support ship had tangled the cable to the ROV in the stern thrusters as it was lowered from the side of the ship. There was a danger that the vehicle and 3 miles of cable may suddenly crash down on top of them, so with that in mind the first dive of the new century ended early.

The *Mir*s were launched on double dives, slowly gathering the items on their recovery list and having them taken back to the surface, where the teams on board the *Keldysh* gently placed them into storage for the journey back to shore. When David Concannon descended on another dive, he spotted a leather bag in the debris field. Bags had been recovered before, but this one was slightly open; as it was recovered, a page from a book became visible, last held by 17-year-old Edgar Samuel Andrew from Argentina, who did not survive the sinking. Another bag recovered on this expedition was owned by First Officer William Murdoch, the man on watch at the time the *Titanic* struck the iceberg. He had packed this bag in the event that he had to escape into a lifeboat; instead, he died in the sinking.

The most incredible of these recoveries were sixty-five vials of perfume, the property of first-class passenger Adolphe Saafield, who lived in Manchester in northern England. Amazingly, the aroma of the perfume filled the air in the conservation laboratory on shore when they were opened after eighty-eight years.

One of those involved in this year's dives was the treasure hunter and explorer Patrick Clyne, who had worked closely with Mel Fisher, the man who spent years searching Caribbean waters for the wreck of the Spanish treasure ship *Nuestra Senora de Atocha*. Fisher was convinced he would find the missing vessel and its riches, the *Atocha* having sunk in a storm in 1622. However, tragedy struck in 1975 when one of his dive boats sank, killing his wife, son and a fellow diver. Even this did not stop his search, and by the mid-1980s he had uncovered $400 million of treasure, making Fisher world famous.

When Fisher died in 1998, Clyne was given the opportunity to visit the wreck of the *Titanic*. He wanted to fix a memorial plaque to the wreck in memory of Fisher. However, Fisher's daughter gave Clyne some of her father's ashes and suggested that they be placed on the wreck. Making the dive in *Mir 2*, Clyne carefully put the ashes on the bridge of the wreck in a clear acrylic container alongside a commemorative medallion. He had given his friend one last dive with him in the most extraordinary way. The strange part of this is that Mel Fisher had absolutely no link to the *Titanic*.

Once the expedition was over, more legal wrangling took place as RMS Titanic Inc was subject to a corporate takeover. In July of that year, the company informed the courts that it planned to sell all its artefacts to the newly formed company The Titanic Foundation Inc. However, this was rejected by the US District Court for the Eastern District of Virginia, which reminded them that RMS Titanic Inc was prohibited from selling any artefacts by the court order from six years before.

In the meantime, Deep Ocean Expeditions returned to the wreck site on 30 August 2000. They carried out ten dives – two a day for five days – until 6 September, using the *Mir* subs. Amongst those visiting the site was shipwreck expert James Delgado, who had published a number of fascinating books about wrecks from the American Civil War and had appeared in a number of TV documentaries.

A report by CBC News said that during one of these dives, a reporter named Michael Guillen was on board one of the submersibles and exploring the debris field when the undersea currents suddenly sent them racing across the seabed, with pilot Viktor Nischeta struggling to retain control. Seconds later, the sub struck one of the *Titanic*'s propellers, pieces of rust flying all around the sub and the impact causing the underwater craft to be jammed under the *Titanic*'s stern. After an hour of rocking the sub back and forth, they were finally able to float free and return unharmed to the surface.

15

GETTING MARRIED AS THE WORLD CHANGED (2001)

FOLLOWING THE HUGE success of the movie *Titanic*, James Cameron was determined to bring the world another look at the wreck of the lost ship. He had already put plans in place for a return to the Atlantic on board the *Keldysh*, bringing with him his friend, actor Bill Paxton, who played the part of fictional salvager Brock Lovett in the film and was about to provide the narration for Cameron's latest offering. Once again diving in the *Mir* submersibles, this was an unusual expedition even for someone like Cameron. Giving Deep Ocean Exploration a call, the expedition was organized and set for August 2001. In the meantime, DOE had two other expeditions to the wreck already arranged, the first dives taking place on 19 July. This time, more oceanographic and shipwreck influencing people were taking advantage of the chance to go back to the depths of the ocean. Don Walsh was a US Navy captain who in 1960 had made the world's first dive to the deepest point in the ocean – the Mariana Trench. Going 7 miles deep, the bathyscaphe *Trieste* made Walsh and his dive partner, Swiss oceanographer Jacques Piccard, world famous. Even today, few expeditions have reached this point on the planet. Now, on 20 July 2001, he was on board the *Keldysh* to make a dive to the *Titanic*, one of many amazing dives he undertook in a lifetime of deep ocean exploration.

Three days of diving were carried out until 22 July, when the *Keldysh* concluded the expedition. Only a week later, the research

Steve Rigby dives the *Titanic* for the first time in the 2001 expedition. (Sue Miller)

ship was back with a new group of people who wanted to explore the wreck. The DOE-led expedition was bringing people who had won a competition by company Subsea Explorer, but they came under fire from some, who branded it a spectacle when a young American couple,

Kimberley Miller and David Leibowitz, arranged to get married inside one of the submersibles while it sat on the deck of the *Titanic*. On the day of the dive, *Mir 2* was not launched, leaving just *Mir 1* with the two passengers and pilot Anatoly Sagalevich in control. The submersible gently landed on the deck of the *Titanic*, and the couple, on their knees in the tiny sub, listened over the radio as the vows were read from the *Keldysh* by Ron Warwick, a Cunard officer and captain of the liner *Queen Elizabeth 2*. They exchanged their vows and were pronounced man and wife, but following the dive came the expected backlash. Relatives of those who died on board *Titanic* criticized the ceremony as being in bad taste, and they were joined by maritime historians who also showed their displeasure. The couple ignored the negative comments, the groom telling the press that any church wedding would be next to a graveyard, so what was the difference? Nonetheless, Brian Ticehurst of the British Titanic Society called it an insult to the victims.

The following day, 29 July, it was the turn of another man who had a huge interest in the wreck, having been fascinated with it since he was a young boy.

It was in 1997 that I (the author) had the privilege to attend the British Titanic Society's annual convention in Southampton, where, as a 16-year-old, I met some likeminded people, some really great *Titanic* experts and even the last living survivor, Millvina Dean. Someone who really made that weekend for me was Steve Rigby, a man obsessed with the *Titanic* and whose enthusiasm was infectious.

The excitement at being in the presence of so many people with the same interest as me was brilliant. Seeing Rigby for the first time and introducing myself to him was a memorable event. When, at this first meeting, I asked him, 'So, what have you got on *Titanic* then?' he simply replied, 'Everything!'

I was very much inclined to believe him!

Stephen William Rigby was born on 12 March 1959, son of William and Hilda Rigby and brother to Sue and Denise. He attended St Mary's Catholic School in Astley, near Manchester and had been researching the sinking of the *Titanic* since the age of 8, when a cousin had shown him a copy of the bestselling Walter Lord book *A Night to Remember*. From that moment on, he was hooked.

As the years went by, Rigby became more fascinated with the story and help set up the British Titanic Society with a number of other like-minded people in 1987, taking on the role of secretary. The doors that opened up for him were phenomenal, as people from all over the world joined the society, attracting some very important *Titanic*-related people into the mix. Soon he would rub shoulders with survivors and relatives of those who had been on board, building these friendships at the annual British Titanic Society conventions, at one of which I met him all those years ago.

Titanic was more than just an interesting subject to Steve Rigby. He would take to heart the commemorations and remembrances, would become angry at the conspiracy theories that were thought up regarding the claim that *Olympic* was really *Titanic*, loudly voicing his opinion that such claims were preposterous.

Then one day in 2001, while carrying out his day job as a postman in Lowton, Greater Manchester, Rigby found out he had won a competition to dive the wreck himself. It was a dream come true. Heading out to the site of his childhood passion aboard the *Keldysh*, he boarded the submersible *Mir 1* for a life-changing dive to the most famous shipwreck in history.

On 29 July 2001, he made is descent to the wreck site. Things became a bit hairy when the sub collided with *Mir 2*, but no damage was caused and they could continue. This had not been the first bit of bad luck during the journey for Rigby, as his luggage containing two memorial plaques to lay on the wreck had not followed him across the Atlantic and was instead still at Heathrow Airport. Thankfully, it was found and sent after him just in time – fifteen minutes before the *Keldysh* sailed for the wreck.

Rigby found his six-hour dive on the wreck a breath-taking experience for him, and he returned with many incredible memories, becoming only the sixty-second person ever to dive down to see the *Titanic*. With him in the submersible that day was another man whose family had a huge part to play in the *Titanic* story. Philip Littlejohn became the first family member of someone who was on board *Titanic* to make the dive to this sacred place. His grandfather was First-Class Steward Alexander Littlejohn, who survived the sinking, rowing away in lifeboat number 13 before being rescued. Alexander Littlejohn died in 1949, but his memory has been honoured in the research carried out by his grandson, who wrote his life story and had now dived the wreck.

Following five days of successful dives, another expedition was over. Nine dives took eighteen more people to the *Titanic*, and with a headline-making wedding controversy as well as Steve Rigby's life-changing dive, it had been another memorable expedition for DOE.

Two weeks later, *Keldysh* was back at the site again, test dives being carried out on 16 and 18 August before passengers were allowed on board. This time it was the return of director James Cameron. He now wanted his record-breaking movie to be followed up by a documentary showing new footage and clear video of the inside of the wreck in a TV special that would attract worldwide attention. With Cameron and actor friend Bill Paxton were artist Ken Marschall, ocean explorer Don Lynch and a host of other *Titanic* experts eager to learn more about the shipwreck.

However, the world changed in the middle of the expedition. On 11 September, the *Mir* submersibles returned to the *Keldysh* to hear that terrorists had attacked New York and Washington. The twin towers of the World Trade Centre had been struck by hijacked aircraft and collapsed, and the Pentagon had been hit in much the same way. Hijackers on a fourth aircraft were tackled by the passengers, and it plunged into a field before it could find its target. What became known as 9/11, the September 11th attacks happened during the filming of Cameron's documentary, the crew hearing about it as they climbed out of the hatch of the submersible back on deck. Although the two terrible events happened almost ninety years apart, people received the news of the tragedies in the same way – with shock, anger, sadness and an immediate desire to know more information.

During this expedition, the *Keldysh* twice returned to St John's in Newfoundland. The expedition was not without other issues. The ROV named *Ellwood* had several problems, firstly getting stuck in the wreck, meaning *Jake*, the second ROV, had to launch a recovery mission. Another time, the ROVs had mechanical failures, but thankfully, before this happened, Cameron was able to get the footage he required in order to complete his work. The expedition was complete by 24 September after twelve successful double dives, each one with Cameron taking high-quality 3D imagery ready to be turned into the upcoming documentary *Ghosts of the Abyss*. Upon release, it was a huge success, also being turned into a 3D IMAX film which provided a whole new cinematic adventure for those eager to lap up anything *Titanic*. It was officially released at the 2003 Cannes Film Festival and had a total worldwide gross of $28.8 million. The footage of inside the wreck was breathtaking, and the film scored many positive reviews from moviegoers and *Titanic* fanatics worldwide.

In the meantime, in November 2001, the Convention on the Protection of the Underwater Cultural Heritage was formally adopted by the United Nations Educational, Scientific and Cultural Organization (UNESCO), creating a legal framework for the protection of relics such as shipwrecks that have been underwater for at least one hundred years. The legislation that was written up was not supported by several nations, including the United States and United Kingdom, as there was such a wide interpretation of what became known as underwater cultural heritage.

What became the RMS *Titanic* Maritime Memorial Act 1986 had been introduced to the US House of Representatives as soon as the wreck was located. It was designed to protect the wreck, involving the cooperation of countries such as the UK, France and Canada, due to them having the deep-water ability to access the wreck, as well as those with a vested interest in the shipwreck for their own various reasons. At no point could RMS Titanic Inc penetrate the wreck to locate and recover items.

An argument raised on many occasions, especially by those considered '*Titanic* tourists', was that the *Titanic* was a British ship in international waters, so at no point should a court in the United States have any jurisdiction over the ship when it had nothing to do with the wreck, nor was it in US territorial waters; if anything, it was closer to Canada than any other nation.

16

NOAA (2003)

THE NATIONAL OCEANIC and Atmospheric Administration (NOAA) is a United States scientific agency dedicated to the oceans and weather. It is, as many documentary filmmakers say, the ocean's version of NASA. Officially formed in 1970, the organization has carried out many expeditions to monitor and explore the deep sea. In 2003, it organized an expedition to explore the wreck of the *Titanic*. The agency's office at Deep Ocean Exploration led the team that hired the Russian research vessel *Akademik Mstislav Keldysh* along with its two *Mir* submersibles. The *Mir* vessels were by now a common sight in *Titanic* documentaries as they were still amongst very few submersibles that could reach the depth at which lay the wreck of the *Titanic*. NOAA was no stranger to shipwreck exploration. Only twelve months before, it had successfully documented, surveyed and salvaged the revolving gun on the wreck of the American Civil War ironclad USS *Monitor* off the coast of North Carolina. And in 2001, it had located the wreck of the submarine *S-5* off New Jersey, where it had gone down in 1920.

On 22 June 2003, the latest expedition headed out to survey the *Titanic* wreck. The team planned to have eleven days at the site, where a number of dives would take place for scientific observations. Also on hand were an expert who had experience in monitoring the Pearl Harbor wreck of the USS *Arizona* and Dr George Bass, who had carried out extensive work in marine archaeology.

Launching the *Mir* submersibles during the 2003 expedition to the *Titanic* wreck site. (NOAA)

As the *Mir* submersibles made their dives, detailed photographs were taken of the stern section to properly map the state of the wreck. Over the coming days, a photographic mosaic was created of the area to form a better understanding of the whole site. A more detailed look was to be taken at the rusticles, which had been observed over the years but it was now felt that further tests needed to be carried out on them.

Beside the scientific nature of their work, those in the submersibles were still in awe of the fact that they were exploring the world's most famous shipwreck of all time. NOAA later released images of

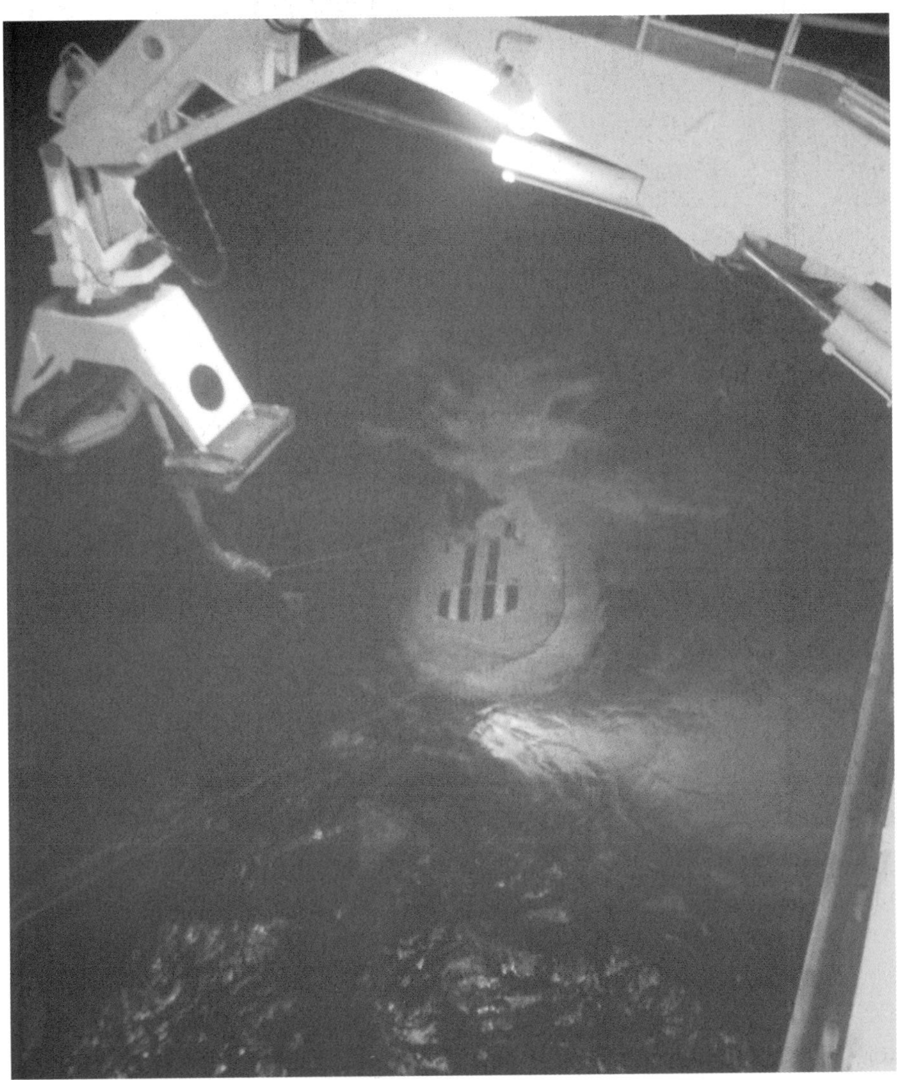

Launching the *Mir* submersibles during the 2003 expedition to the wreck of the *Titanic*. (NOAA)

the bathtub in Captain Smith's cabin, and the latest video footage increased understanding of the deterioration rates of the shipwreck. The latest research, in particular microbiological analysis of the wreck, would also be used when they went back to their labs on dry land. All in all, the expedition proved a huge success, contributing to NOAA's understanding of the marine life in and around the wreck site. Upon the completion of all their on-site investigations, the *Keldysh* returned to port on 2 July.

Subsequently, more than two hours of new wreck footage was released to the world's media, showing the bow section and close-up views of the anchor crane, upper deck structure, funnel openings and the hull itself. A number of still images were also released to accompany the video footage. However, perhaps because no sensational stories or controversies accompanied this expedition, there was a lot less media focus on its results than on other dives.

The *Mir* crews pose for a photograph during the 2003 expedition. (NOAA)

One of those on board the *Mir 2* for this trip was TV documentary host and diver Carl Spencer, who had a major interest in the *Titanic* and its sister ship, *Britannnic*. Tragically, Carl would lose his life during a dive on *Britannnic* six year later.

DOE was not finished yet with the wreck site, organizing a return to the *Titanic* for two more day's diving on 5 and 7 July this year, again for private viewings. The *Keldysh* then again went back to port to be readied for its next expedition to a deep-sea site, another one of James Cameron's projects, this time nowhere near the *Titanic*.

Captain Smith's bathroom on *Titanic*, seen in 2003. (NOAA)

Above: Rusticles hang from the wreck during the 2003 expedition. (NOAA)

Left: Night-time recovery of the *Mir* submersibles in 2003. (NOAA)

Launching one of the *Mir*s in 2003. (NOAA)

17

BALLARD RETURNS (2004)

BY NOW IT was eighteen years since Robert Ballard had last visited the wreck in the *Alvin*, but he was planning a new expedition to see how the site had changed during that time, and what the rates of deterioration were, on behalf of the National Oceanic and Atmospheric Administration. Again, he would be taking no artefacts. Indeed, due to advances in technology, there was by now no need for a human being to actually dive down to the seabed; they could easily watch video footage live from a remotely operated vehicle from the safety of a control room. Since he had located the *Titanic* in 1985, Ballard had gone on to discover numerous famous shipwrecks using these types of ROVs, putting no human lives at risk from a potential incident. He had successfully located wrecks from Guadalcanal, the *Bismarck*, Roman and Phoenician wrecks, John F. Kennedy's *PT-109* and the USS *Yorktown*, and had also explored both the *Lusitania* and *Britannic*. His discovery of the *Titanic* had opened up all these opportunities for him.

For his return to *Titanic* he chartered the *Ronald H. Brown*, a 274-ft-long research vessel of 3,180 gross tons, built for NOAA by Halter Marine of Pascagoula, Mississippi. The *Ronald H. Brown* (IMO Number 9105786) was named after the US Secretary of Commerce who had died in a plane crash in 1996 and was launched on 30 May that year, just a month after his death. It was originally going to be named *Researcher,* but this was changed at the last minute

The NOAA research vessel *Ronald H. Brown* that Ballard used for his 2004 return to the wreck, seen here launching *Jason*, another of Ballard's vehicles from a different expedition. (NOAA)

to honour Brown's memory. On 19 July 1997, the *Ronald H. Brown* was commissioned by NOAA into its fleet, with room for twenty-six crew and thirty-two scientists. It boasted a hospital facility as well as a variety of equipment to conduct surveys and deep-ocean exploration. One of three sister ships built generally to the same design, expeditions were soon coming thick and fast for the ship, but it would now become involved in the story of the *Titanic*.

The *Ronald H. Brown* sailed into the Atlantic in May 2004, and Ballard was once again on a wave of publicity, the press following his every move as the ship returned to the discovery that had made him a household name. Using his latest ROV, *Hercules*, the images he brought back were in high definition. The quality was so much better than anything he could have ever wished for back in 1985, when he was first passing over the wreck site with *Argo* and *ANGUS*. While the *Ronald H. Brown* was on site, the expedition was broadcast live to schoolchildren throughout the United States. Via a brainchild that Ballard had developed in the 1980s that was now called Telepresence, students were able to control equipment on the ship from thousands of miles away in a classroom. The opportunity to learn about the oceans was always at the forefront of these expeditions, which had been Ballard's dream long before the discovery of the *Titanic*.

For the next eleven days, the team worked on making a detailed map of the ship while scientifically analysing the surroundings, beginning work on 30 May, three days after they had set sail from the mainland. The team consisted of engineers and scientists, including Roy Cullimore, who specialised in microbial research and was keen to see how the rusticles formed from tiny microbes that feed on the iron. Rusticles was a term invented by Ballard on the first expeditions, when he noticed that rust was 'dripping' down the hull and hanging

The NOAA research vessel *Ronald H. Brown* used by Ballard for his return to the wreck in 2004. (NOAA)

like icicles. At this point, very little was known about what made this happen; they also wanted to learn more about how this had affected the wreck, particularly the speed at which it was helping the hull deteriorate. This information could be used to further their research regarding other shipwrecks and submerged cultural resources, but it also gave Ballard an opportunity to revisit his discovery and see for himself how *Titanic* had changed over the last two decades.

During the expedition there was a live broadcast by the National Geographic television channel, with exclusive access to the wreck exploration, being beamed direct from the *Ronald H. Brown* to TV screens. The one-hour broadcast was aptly named *Return to Titanic*. Several more live broadcasts allowed children around the United States to participate in the mission, continuing work that Ballard's JASON Foundation had been doing for more than fifteen years. Back in 1989, he had live link-ups from the Mediterranean to children around the world who asked questions while work was carried out on the wreck of a Roman ship he had named *Isis*. He shared images and information about the artefacts with excited audiences, and he hoped the *Titanic* expedition would prove even more popular. His ROV at the time of the *Isis* expeditions, *Jason*, was the predecessor to his new *Hercules*, which featured some of the latest technological advances.

The expedition was a huge success, results of investigations showing considerable deterioration of the hull caused by submarines from previous expeditions landing on the decks, the numerous salvage operations and the general wear and tear caused by nearly two decades more of sea life and strong currents. There were clear marks on the hull where submersibles had landed on the deck and scraped along the surface. Comparing his images from 1986 with those from 2004, Ballard could show that there was a huge change in the wreck, meaning that previous estimates of when the hull might eventually collapse would have to be revised. Ballard noticed so many changes himself: the mast had collapsed, the crow's nest was long gone, parts of the upper deck were now obscured and thousands of items from the debris field had been salvaged.

The expedition was completed on 9 June and returned to port three days later, following which the scientists pored over their findings for many months. Ballard was interviewed numerous times about his findings, and his book and the National Geographic documentary, both called *Return to Titanic*, were very popular.

The *Ronald H. Brown*, meanwhile, returned to other expeditions. On 18 July 2013, the ship sailed from its home port of Charleston, South Carolina, on a mission that would become the longest deployment in the history of NOAA, not returning until 25 May 2017. During that time, it travelled 130,000 nautical miles and spent nearly 800 days at sea. The studies that took place and the amount of data collected contributed to huge advances in scientific knowledge, this marathon trip making the headlines upon the vessel's return.

Robert Ballard will always be known as the greatest-ever shipwreck hunter, his discovery of the *Titanic* and *Bismarck* cementing his name in the history books. Since his last trip to the *Titanic*, he has carried on his deep-ocean exploration. His legacy lives on in the Institute for Exploration, an organisation that he set up to explore the deep seas using a research vessel that he aptly named *Nautilus* after his favourite fictional submarine in Jules Verne's novel *20,000 Leagues Under the Sea*. In 2019, he launched an expedition to search for the wreckage of the aircraft of missing aviator Amelia Earhart; while he did not locate the plane, the team worked through a lot of evidence and found out where the wreckage was not, thereby ending much speculation.

Ballard's was not the only expedition to the *Titanic* wreck site in 2004, as later that year RMS Titanic Inc launched their seventh expedition to the location. On this occasion there were no manned submersibles used; instead, they utilized a ROV provided by Phoenix International Inc. There were still recovery operations taking place, and items taken from the site included a Turkish bath tile frame and a gilded wall sconce from the À la carte restaurant.

Whilst at the site, the RMS Titanic Inc team retrieved a set of racks of corrosion coupons that had been placed near the wreck six years before during the 1998 expedition. They had been left here as an experiment to determine the weight loss and levels of corrosion in the environmental surroundings of the wreck. Samples of the rusticles were taken for further analysis and compared to the rust on previous tests carried out on six shipwrecks from the Second World War that were resting in the much shallower Gulf of Mexico. The results showed a clear correlation between water depth and rusticle formation: the deeper the water, the larger the rust formation. A 1996 survey had concluded that around 650 tons of rusticles had formed on the bow section of *Titanic* alone. The ocean currents had deposited the iron elements, and over time had made the rusticles develop; the ship now almost looked to be alive with these iron deposits.

The NOAA research vessel *Ronald H. Brown* that Ballard used for his 2004 return to the wreck. (NOAA)

18

CAMERON RETURNS (2005)

AFTER THE MASSIVE success of his movie *Titanic* and documentary *Ghosts of the Abyss*, film director James Cameron was anxious to return to the wreck site. He announced plans to make several more trips to *Titanic* using the *Mir* submersibles to bring back some of the most incredible footage of the site ever seen, using remotely operated vehicles to film deep inside the wreck and once again have *Titanic* on the big screen. Launching his fact-finding mission in 2005, he contacted Deep Ocean Expeditions, who organized the *Keldysh* to be at Cameron's disposal, sailing from Kaliningrad in the Baltic on 28 May 2005. It then spent a week above the wreck site in early June, the director going down in the submersibles in five double dives.

Releasing small ROVs to go further into the wreck than ever before, Cameron's use of technology was again proving that there was still much to explore within the companionways and cabins, as the never-before-seen Turkish baths were filmed, along with ghostly corridors and staircases deep inside the remains of the bow section. With parts of the ship having never been photographed, nobody really knew just what some of these compartments looked like; they could only rely on diagrams and what had been written about them. Cameron's filming finally revealed the sumptuous colours of the tiles on the walls of the Turkish baths.

Another trip to the *Titanic* took place less than a week after the Cameron expedition had ended, when members of DOE were given the opportunity to visit the wreck themselves. Five double dives took place between 10 and 15 July before the *Keldysh* was back working with Cameron again on 21 July for four more dives to complete his filming.

A very busy year at the wreck site saw two more expeditions in the August, with a number of *Titanic* experts, artists, filmmakers and divers making the perilous journey down to see the wreck. Each double dive went off as planned, involving a further sixteen launches of the *Mir* submersibles between 3 and 15 August before the season was finally done for the year. When the survey ship arrived at St Johns on 18 August, after just under three months at sea, the dives to the *Titanic* had allowed dozens more people to have the opportunity to visit the wreck.

Meanwhile, back on shore, Cameron's team was hard at work with the footage that he had captured during his dives. His new

Richie Kohler makes his first dive to the wreck in 2005. (Richie Kohler)

documentary, *Last Mysteries of the Titanic*, was a resounding success, a perfect ending to Cameron's three major filming expeditions that had taken him a decade to complete. This was the same year that Cameron's IMAX movie *Aliens of the Deep* was released, with incredible footage of his visit to the mid-ocean ridges of both the Atlantic and Pacific.

Cameron was certainly bitten by the deep-ocean bug. Since his dives started on *Titanic*, he has become one of only a few people to have also descended into the Mariana Trench in the Pacific and been down to the wreck of the German battleship *Bismarck*. His film successes since he released *Titanic* have included the smash-hit *Avatar*, co-creating the sci-fi series *Dark Angel* and working on sequels to both *Avatar* and *Terminator*. He has also worked extensively on documentaries, especially surrounding the *Titanic* and

Richie Kohler takes a photo of the wreck through the *Mir* viewport, showing the numerous plaques that have been left on the bridge area. (Richie Kohler)

the oceans, working with TV presenter Tony Robinson and Dr Robert Ballard for other *Titanic* wreck-related programmes, a subject that clearly will always be close to his heart.

Despite his success on the wreck and with other exploration expeditions, Cameron has spoken out on the dangers of visiting deep-sea wrecks. During his thirty-three dives to the *Titanic*, he has been involved in numerous incidents, with submersibles colliding with the wreck or being stuck on the seabed, each time the dive being aborted or ending earlier than expected. Eighteen years later, the danger of not heeding his warnings about repeatedly visiting a wreck of this magnitude were proved in the most tragic of circumstances.

James Cameron was not the only person to dive the *Titanic* in 2005. Steve Rigby, who had first made the trip in 2001, also returned to the wreck. Together with Brigitte Saar, he published a book on their diving experience in 2006, titled *The Ultimate Experience – Our Dive to the Titanic*.

Steve continued to be active within the British Titanic Society for many years. Together they hosted conventions in various *Titanic*-related locations, including Halifax, Nova Scotia, to where many victims of the disaster had been brought and where several are now laid to rest.

Another one of the passengers in the *Mir* submersibles for the August 2005 expedition to *Titanic* was Richie Kohler, a diver who had made a name for himself in the TV series *Deep Sea Detectives*, a popular shipwreck diving documentary programme shown on the History Channel. Growing up watching the footage of the Apollo moon landings, Kohler quickly saw the parallels between an astronaut and an aquanaut. With a keen interest in shipwrecks and the ability to explore the deep seas, he soon learned to dive. He found that dive sites around the world were literally time capsules, from which he could learn so much. He took part in a dive on the wreck of the Italian liner *Andrea Doria*, and was more than familiar with the story of the sinking of the *Titanic*.

Kohler's free time was spent researching lost ships and carrying out more diving whenever he could, and he soon found himself on camera hosting *Deep Sea Detectives*, making a living showing his passion for solving undersea mysteries and delving into the maritime history of the world's lost ships. By the third season of the show, a new idea was pitched to send its stars to the wreck of the *Titanic*, but they found that the price just to charter the *Keldysh* was astronomical. Nevertheless, together with co-host John Chatterton he eventually made it happen, in what remains to this day the most expensive diving expedition they have ever undertaken.

Setting sail from Newfoundland with around twenty others – six of them being his film crew – Kohler and his team spent the time wisely, interviewing people on board the *Keldysh* after already using time ashore to photograph the graves of *Titanic* victims in Halifax and checking out the technological marvels they would be using to go down to the wreck site. With them were a number of *Titanic* experts, along with some of the wives of those making the trip. Preparations had begun many months beforehand, the team reading up on everything *Titanic*-related so that they were familiar with all aspects of the story. For Kohler, this was in many ways no different to the other shipwreck dives he had done, only this time it was the most famous wreck in the world, and of course a lot deeper and more dangerous.

Although he had been in a submersible before, Kohler had never descended to anywhere near this depth. Despite him being a veteran of diving on historic wrecks, he was thus restless in his bed on the *Keldysh* the night before as the excitement and anticipation had his adrenaline working overtime. The next day, despite lack of sleep, he was buzzing as he climbed aboard *Mir 2* and lowered himself into the small sphere where the three people squashed together ready for the off. With a jerk, the submersible was lifted using the

The final dive of the *Mir 2* submersible on the wreck of *Titanic* in 2005. The subs were retired soon after. (David Concannon)

ship's crane and was swung out over the side. A slight lurch signified their entry into the cold Atlantic, with the 'cowboy' above, riding the submersible, detaching the connecting cable before a small boat pulled him clear and the submersible was free to dive.

Excited at the prospect of the wreck being only hours away, Kohler pressed his face against the view port as the light slowly faded and darkness enveloped them. Within minutes, he had already reached the maximum depth he had ever gone as a scuba diver. Inside the vessel, the technology around them was making its own unique sounds, the whirring and clicking of instruments signifying that all was well. Ralph White, the *National Geographic* cameraman, was just as excited, but he nodded off, as did the pilot, Genya Cherniaev. Kohler was too pumped up to rest, his thoughts racing as the anticipation of what he was about to see darted through his mind.

After descending for more than two hours, the pilot slowed the submersible and they were soon at the grey seafloor. Cherniaev

Rob McCallum diving during the 2005 expedition. (Rob McCallum)

navigated the *Mir 2* towards the bow of the *Titanic*; all Richie could say was, 'Oh my God! Unbelievable!', as the famous liner came into view. The submersible slowly moved around the familiar fo'c'sle area, and before long several hours had passed, the sight of the wreck being so overwhelming for him that he lost track of time. As they headed out into the debris field and towards the stern, the inside of the *Mir 2* was freezing cold, condensation having started to build up on the sides of the inner sphere, pooling into a small bilge below their feet.

While passing over the wreckage of the stern, Kohler contemplated just what had gone on here ninety-three years ago, terrified people clinging on to this last area of the ship above the water in a desperate bid to stay alive. It was a sad moment, leaving him with a sense of melancholy as the dive ended and the submersible headed back to the surface.

The team's third dive was Kohler's second visit to the wreck; it was a race against time to get on camera the areas of the debris field that had led them to be part of this expedition in the first place. With little time to spare, the submersible discovered two huge sections of the *Titanic*'s double-bottom hull, a complete section from port to starboard, even including the red anti-fouling paint still clinging to the surface. For Kohler, this was a marvellous find to get on camera, one that he could now take back to the documentary team.

Richie Kohler and John Chatterton went on to produce four series of *Deep Sea Detectives*, visiting many more shipwrecks and solving various historical mysteries along the way. He was good friends with fellow diver Carl Spencer, and was with him on *Britannic* when he died in 2009. Since visiting the *Titanic*, Kohler has organized nine expeditions to the wreck of its sister ship, also producing a book and movie on the wreck of the German submarine *U-869*.

The Deep Ocean Exploration company had now spent seven years carrying out a number of expeditions, organizing private dives on the wreck, and this year they decided that it was time to discontinue the venture. Instead, they would promote the thrill of heading to other deep-diving destinations for ocean tourists. By the time the ventures to *Titanic* ended this year, the cost had almost doubled for tourists wanting to make the journey. Rob McCallum would be called upon to make other trips to various exciting locations around the world, such as the deep see vents in the Mid-Atlantic Ridge and the wreck of the *Bismarck*.

Because DOE were the commercial managers of the expeditions, they did not broadcast their involvement in the press. Each client was there for their own reasons, and would release their own documentary or book, leaving the hard work done by McCallum and his team in the background, with all the attention on people like James Cameron for their incredible film footage and the crews of the *Keldysh*. Many of the people who subsequently had their names and faces plastered all over the press actually did very little when it came to the arranging of the expeditions – they would simply get in the submersible and enjoy the dive. Then again, they had paid thousands of dollars to make these trips, and the expeditions would otherwise never have taken place.

The by now world-famous research vessel *Akademik Mstislav Keldysh* went on to make other major visits to deep-water sites, including the *Bismarck* for another Cameron special as well as the Japanese submarine *I-52*. Between 2008 and 2010, the two *Mir* subs were exploring the largest freshwater lake in the world, Lake Baikal in Russia, at one point being joined by the then Prime Minister of Russia, Vladimir Putin. The year after that expedition, they were diving Lake Geneva. After fascinating careers that have gone down in history for several reasons, the *Mir 1* and *Mir 2* were eventually decommissioned in 2017, ending thirty years of hard work. They were then laid up at the PP Shirshov Institute in Moscow and are no longer operational. The 2005 dives to *Titanic* with Richie Kohler and his team were the last time the *Mir* submersibles would go down to the world's most famous shipwreck.

Due to the nature of the expeditions its crew carried out, the *Keldysh* is now one of the most famous research ships in history, not least because it was featured prominently in the Cameron film. Several major documentaries also propelled it into the annals of undersea exploration history. The ship still plies the seas today.

DOE head Rob McCallum is at the time of writing the head of EYOS – Expeditions, Yacht Charters, Operations, Special Projects – which continues to take tourists on unique experiences, from the highest mountains to the deepest points of the ocean, including the Five Deeps Expedition to the bottom of each of the world's five oceans. Collaborating with many other organizations, EYOS was part of a team that discovered the deepest-known shipwreck, that of the destroyer USS *Samuel B Roberts,* which went down in the Battle of Samar in the Philippines on 25 October 1944 and was located in 2022 at a depth of 22,621ft (4.3 miles).

19

RMS *TITANIC* INC EXPEDITION NO 8 (2010)

THE SUMMER OF 2010 saw RMS Titanic Inc return to the wreck. They did not give much information about their aims or what they were planning to do, just saying that they were taking innovative measures 'to virtually raise *Titanic*', it being assumed that they meant digitally rather than physically. Led by David Gallo from Woods Hole and Christopher Davino, president of RMS Titanic Inc, the expedition used two REMUS AUVs (Remote Environmental Measuring Units – Autonomous Underwater Vehicles) named *Ginger* and *Mary Ann*, as well as an ROV called *Remora*. These could be set up and launched in a matter of hours, saving so much more time than a manned mission and producing better results.

Funded by RMS Titanic Inc, they were joined by NOAA, the Office of National Marine Sanctuaries and Woods Hole Oceanographic Institution, who brought along their Advanced Imaging and Visualization Laboratory (AIVL). The vessels would be launched from the research ship *Jean Charcot* (IMO number 6505777), normally engaged in fishery protection duties and registered in the South Pacific islands of Vanuatu. Built by Constructions Industrielles De La Mediterranee Du Havre in Le Havre, France, in 1965, the ship was named after a French neurologist and professor of anatomical pathology, who during his research discovered details about the brain that was pioneering in the analysis of brain haemorrhages. The ship bearing his name weighed 2,141 gross tons and was 243ft long, with a large yellow A-frame on the stern that allowed the launch of the underwater vehicles that would survey the *Titanic*.

These were deployed to map the wreck and scan over the debris field, focussing on some of the wider-spread wreckage further away from the main site – loose items and pieces of hull that had scattered in a larger area when the ship had gone down. Some of the items were 'tagged' so that specific features could be identified and the seabed examined to see how it had interacted with the descent of the ship hitting the mud. They could also use this data to plan future dives for further research and assess whether damage had taken place over that time or if any artefacts had been removed without authorization. The AUVs and ROV got to work to map a 10 square mile section of the seabed, taking in the entire wreck site.

These sonar scans were overlaid with photographs of the wreck, which led to a huge map of the entire area being developed. The work required to put all this together would take many months to complete and result in possibly several years' worth of study by analysts and experts.

One of the things highlighted on this survey was the 70ft section of the hull that was no longer connected (the part between the main bow section and the stern), much of which had been found on previous expeditions, as well as some of the machinery from inside this part of the ship that had been scattered all around the same area. It was said that although this missing section accounted for only 10 per cent of the wreck, it was the source of almost everything that lay scattered around the site. This meant that the internal parts of the two large sections of the *Titanic* were theoretically intact inside.

This was the first time that every single visible piece of wreckage could be mapped, seen and studied for later examination without a single human being descending to the seabed or any artefacts being taken. What was observed, though, was the amount of human materiel from modern times now littering the wreck, with at least five memorial plaques, the ashes of treasure hunter Mel Fisher, an American flag, plastic flowers, submersible ballast weights (dropped in order for them to resurface) and even everyday garbage such as disposable cups; all were now lodged within the wreckage and surrounding debris field. At this point, the issue was raised as to whether there should be an exclusion zone around the wreck site to end the problem of garbage being left. This would also include having specific zones for the submersibles to land and ascend, with weights dropped away from the *Titanic*. What was more concerning was the amount of everyday rubbish that was in the ocean, having drifted hundreds of miles from the nearest land. David Gallo released a photograph to the media of a plastic bag floating in the ocean close to the research vessel.

The expedition then had to be cut short, as Hurricane Danielle started to make headway towards the team. The *Jean Charcot* recovered the vehicles and headed back to Newfoundland. The ship went alongside for a week, before heading out to the wreck site again. Unfortunately, a second hurricane brought proceedings to a definitive end just over a week later. Nevertheless, during that time they managed to get plenty of survey work completed, the results of which would change how future expeditions visited the wreck.

All the work from the expedition culminated in the documentary *RMS Titanic: 100 Years in 3D*, featuring the latest footage that had been shot. The images of the overlays would then be released to the world via *National Geographic* magazine, which featured the sunken liner once again in its 100th anniversary issue. Eventually, the images were collated into an incredible 250-part mosaic of the wreck site.

The fishery protection vessel *Jean Charcot* continues conducting survey work to this day, having been in service around the globe constantly in the sixty years since being launched.

20

CENTENARY (2012)

THE SITE OF THE *TITANIC* wreck was the scene for a different type of expedition in 2012 when the 100th anniversary of the disaster was approaching. Over a year in advance of the date, Fred Olsen Cruises was advertising a memorial cruise to the location of the *Titanic* disaster on board the *Balmoral*, chartered by Miles Morgan Travel, which would follow the original route from Southampton, sailing past Cherbourg and Cobh (formerly known as Queenstown) before heading into the mid-Atlantic to the wreck site.

At 714ft 11in long and weighing 43,537 gross tons, the *Balmoral* (IMO Number 8506294) had already been enjoyed by thousands of travellers in the two decades before this centenary trip. While a small cruise liner in comparison to the huge more modern ships, it she was still a favourite for many regular travellers. The *Balmoral* started out as the *Crown Odyssey* when launched on 1 November 1987 from the Meyer Werft shipyard in Papenburg, West Germany, and was handed over to owners Royal Cruise Line and named on 14 May 1988. In 1992, it was bought by Norwegian Cruise Line and renamed *Norwegian Crown* four years later, before reverting to *Crown Odyssey* in 2000 when it was operated by Orient Lines. Renamed yet again in 2003, it became the *Norwegian Crown* yet again for four years before its final owners Balmoral Cruise Ltd, operated by Fred Olsen Cruise Line, named it *Balmoral* in 2008, the name it still has at the time of writing.

The liner *Balmoral* visited the wreck site for the 100th anniversary of the disaster and led the commemorations. It is seen here off Tallinn, Estonia, in 2013. (Pjotr Mahhonin)

The vessel has been a popular tourist ship over the years, a sleek white hull giving its port of registration as Nassau when acquired by Balmoral Cruise, with the Fred Olsen logo on the single funnel aft. Its two propellers can power the ship forward at a top speed of 22.5 knots, and its 1,230 passengers on eleven decks (nine of them for the passengers) can be entertained by various activities before they head to the next port of call.

The liner made headlines on 21 January 2009 when it hit rough seas in the Bay of Biscay, an incident that ended up with two of the passengers being seriously injured and having to be taken to a Spanish hospital for treatment.

For the memorial cruise, *Balmoral* sailed on 8 April 2012 and went as scheduled to the ports in the itinerary, arriving at the site of the *Titanic* wreck on 14 April. On board were a number of relatives of the victims, the last survivor having died three years before. The crew dressed in 1912-style period clothing for the theme of the voyage, as did some of the passengers, items on the menu also giving a taste of what was served on board the ill-fated liner a century before.

At the exact position of the wreck, the *Balmoral* stopped in the water at 2300hrs as people gathered for a memorial service on the stern of the ship, remembering those who had died in the sinking. The ship's horn sounded out at almost the exact moment the ship struck the iceberg, and three of the crew members held floral wreaths which were blessed by the ship's padre before being cast into the sea. With commemorations taking place across the globe, the images of the ceremony on *Balmoral* were broadcast live to news outlets on both sides of the Atlantic. A band played in the freezing darkness of the upper deck at the stern of the *Balmoral* as the lives of all those who were lost on board the *Titanic* were commemorated.

After the ceremony, the ship's engines were restarted and the *Balmoral* continued on to New York, the intended final destination of the *Titanic* and the one port of call that it had never made on its first journey.

This would have been a poignant moment for Steve Rigby of the British Titanic Society, who had always wanted to organize something for the 100th anniversary of the disaster. Sadly, he never got the chance as he died on 8 May 2011, at Wigan Infirmary, at the young age of 52. His funeral was held at Howe Bridge Crematorium in Atherton, Lancashire. Nevertheless, his legacy lived on, his family joining those aboard the *Balmoral*, from which his ashes were scatted over the wreck of the *Titanic* during the centenary memorial voyage. It is where he would have wanted to be.

21

LIMITING FACTOR AND THE DSSV *PRESSURE DROP* (2019)

AS COMMERCIAL DIVING became a huge industry over the years, so too did the potential to take private companies, tourists and explorers to the *Titanic* using underwater craft in revolutionary designs and bizarre shapes. In 2019, an expedition was organized utilizing the NOAA-owned DSSV (Deep Submersible Support Vessel) *Pressure Drop* to carry out an exploration of the wreck. At 224ft long and weighing 1,914 gross tons, the vessel was launched by the Tacoma Boatbuilding Co in Washington State, USA on 16 July 1985 as the *USNS Indomitable*, built for the US Navy as a Stalwart-class ocean surveillance ship. It was placed in the non-commissioned section of the Military Sealift Command on 26 November 1985, from where it would sail out to conduct anti-submarine operations during the latter years of the Cold War era. Fitted with a number of sensors, including towed array technology to listen for submarines, the demise of the Soviet Union in 1991 meant that many ships like this were becoming redundant for such roles. Instead, they were taking up the new role of counter-narcotics in the Caribbean.

On 2 December 2002, *Indomitable* was struck from the Naval Vessel Register and officially retired from the US Navy, being acquired by NOAA a week later and renamed *McArthur II*, now assigned to conduct oceanographic research, carrying thirty-eight

DSSV *Pressure Drop* passes an iceberg. (Richard Varcoe on behalf of Caladan Oceanic LLC)

personnel. On board now were laboratories and a refrigerator unit, as well as equipment on the upper deck to conduct vehicle launches when required, quite a change of pace from its Cold War role.

McArthur II conducted many surveys of the US Pacific coast from its home port of Seattle before being retired by NOAA in 2014, by which time it had already been laid up for three years. It was a further three years before Caladan Oceanic LLC purchased the ship for their own expeditions and renamed it the DSSV *Pressure Drop*, a mother ship for their new submersible DSV (Deep Submergence Vehicle) *Limiting Factor*.

Built by Triton Submarines LLC and owned by explorer and businessman Victor Vescovo, the 15ft-long submersible weighed just 12.5 tons. Of all the submersibles in the *Titanic* story, the design of the *Limiting Factor* is quite unusual in the way it looks; it is almost as if mother ship *Pressure Drop* is lowering a large suitcase over the side rather than a sophisticated piece of ocean exploration kit.

Despite appearances, this submersible has been on a number of high-profile deep-water shipwreck exploration missions since it was built in 2018. Also owned by Victor Vescovo, this can only fit two people inside but can dive to 36,000ft for sixteen hours, the only manned submersible at the time of writing that can dive to literally any point in the world's oceans.

The *Limiting Factor*'s remarkable career started with the Five Deeps Expedition, where the exploration team commenced diving serials to the deepest parts of each of the world's oceans, an achievement that was done within a year. During this period, Vescovo became the first person to dive a feature known as the Molloy Deep in the Arctic Ocean.

Then came the moment that made the vessel the star of TV documentaries over the next few years when, in August 2019, it was used on the first expedition to the *Titanic* in fourteen years, bringing back new footage of the wreck and allowing explorers to see the state of decay on the hull compared to the last visit in 2005. During five dives

Limiting Factor on an expedition to the isand of South Georgia. (Richard Varcoe on behalf of Caladan Oceanic LLC)

Limiting Factor prepares for an Atlantic dive. (Richard Varcoe on behalf of Caladan Oceanic LLC)

over the space of eight days, the *Limiting Factor* found that the famous area of the captain's bathtub would never be seen again, as the structure around it had collapsed, burying the bath.

One area of controversy during this visit came when the *Limiting Factor* was caught out by currents and collided with the wreck. It was not so much that any damage was caused to either the *Titanic* or the submersible, but the fact that the event was never mentioned publicly until a year later, leading to allegations of a cover up being thrown around in the press. The collision was openly admitted on a documentary in 2020 and nothing further was mentioned, the public perhaps unaware that collisions with the wreck of the *Titanic* had been going on for many years without any commotion.

A documentary on the expedition largely featured images of experts poring over different areas of the debris field in the hope of identifying areas worth further investigation at a later date. This included a controversial plan to cut open the wreck and retrieve what is left of the Marconi system from the radio room, a huge part of the *Titanic* story in which the ship sent one of the first SOS calls (not the first though, which was from the *Slavonia,* which was wrecked in 1909). At the time of writing, this salvage has still not been carried out.

Once the *Titanic* expedition had been completed, hunts were carried out for further wrecks, utilizing all the latest technology. Later in 2019, the wreck of the USS *Johnston*, sunk in the Battle of Samar in 1944, was thought to have been discovered by a team on board the research vessel *Petrel*. However, attempts to get enough footage to positively identify the wreck of the destroyer failed due to it being at a depth of 20,000ft. *Limiting Factor* was tasked to carry out a survey on the ship in 2021 and successfully confirmed the wreck as that of the *Johnston*, which was at the time the deepest shipwreck ever discovered. That record didn't last long.

In June 2022, it was broken when Vescovo and his team discovered the destroyer USS *Samuel B. Roberts*, sunk in the Battle of Leyte Gulf in 1944, at a new record depth of 22,523ft. The images of both these lost shipwrecks from the Second World War were beamed around the

Limiting Factor floating on the surface. (Richard Varcoe on behalf of Caladan Oceanic LLC)

Pressure Drop launches the sub. (Richard Varcoe on behalf of Caladan Oceanic LLCV)

world, meaning the final resting place of these two relics of the Pacific campaign could now be studied and then allowed to rest in peace.

Another wreck that was located in 2019 was the French submarine *Minerve*, which had vanished with fifty-two crew on board in the western Mediterranean in 1968, a year when four submarines from four different nations sank (the others being the American *Scorpion*, Israeli *Dakar* and Russian *K-129*). The year after the discovery, Vescovo put forward a plan to dive the wreck with a retired French rear admiral, during which they were able to lay a memorial plaque on the stricken sub.

By 2021, after three years of exploration, Victor Vescovo decided to sell his company, and both the DSSV *Pressure Drop* (IMO Number 8833867) and DSV *Limiting Factor* were put up for sale. *Pressure Drop* was bought by ocean exploration company Inkfish, owned by businessman Gabe Newell, and was renamed *Dagon*. At the time of writing, it continues to explore the world's oceans. The *Limiting Factor* was renamed *Bakunawa* and today still carries out dives to the deepest depths of the oceans.

22

MAPPING BY MAGELLAN (2019)

THE SAME YEAR as the *Limiting Factor* expedition, another vessel named *Freja* was preparing to conduct a very different kind of survey on the *Titanic* wreck. This 246ft-long ship was previously the *Grampian Surveyor* (IMO Number 9258533), built in Spain as an offshore oil industry support vessel. It was launched in 2003 from the Astilleros Balenciaga shipyard in Zumaia, Spain, and had a long and successful career serving as a ROV support ship. It was bought by a company named Magellan and renamed in 2016 as *Freja*, sailing under the flag of Denmark. On board was a state-of-the-art dynamic positioning system as well as bow and stern thrusters to keep the ship on station if the sea became rough during operations.

Freja was not a huge ship, but this blue-hulled workhorse of the sea had a large crane aft for the launching of underwater vehicles and the ability to operate in the cold climates of the Baltic as well as the stormy Atlantic. That was just as well, because in the summer of 2019, the *Freja* headed out with an expedition crew to the wreck of the *Titanic* with a very different mission to previous ones to the wreck site.

Magellan is based in Guernsey in the Channel Islands, which had lost a total of twenty-nine people when the *Titanic* had gone down – ten from Jersey and another nineteen from Guernsey. Founded in 2015 by Richard Parkinson, the company, according to their website,

Freja was used for the 2019 mapping expedition by Magellan. It is seen here in 2018. (John D. Durrant)

'is driven by a management team whose background includes offshore contracting, geotechnical survey and ultra-deep water ROV operations, including environmental and site investigation'. While their main clients are normally within the oil and gas industry, they are also hired as underwater recovery specialists as well as assisting in undersea operations within the fibre-optic industries. The relationships that Magellan have fostered over the years have led to them building many connections around the globe and assisting in major projects.

In 2019, Captain Jan Eliassen navigated the *Freja* to the *Titanic* wreck site, where two ROV's named *Romeo* and *Juliet* were lowered into position. A vast array of ground-breaking technology was utilized to digitally scan the wreck over a six-week period until the entire wreck and surrounding debris field – an area of 3 square miles – had been covered from every angle. The intention was to eventually generate a 3D model, with the detail in the images so clear that the yard number '401' was visible on the propeller. The images were taken back to shore and their team of specialists took several years to put together the huge jigsaw. Finally, in May 2023, they were released to the public, causing such a sensation that the *Titanic* was once again back in the headlines. Two submersible craft launched from the *Freja* had been used to capture some 700,000 images, an epic mission with a fascinating result.

Among the incredible discoveries on the expedition was a necklace in the debris field made from the tooth of a megalodon, a shark from prehistoric times, in a gold setting. At the time of writing, researchers from Magellan were still attempting to find out who the necklace belonged to. It was hoped that somebody, somewhere would have a record of such an intricate piece of jewellery, and that they would be able to tell the story of who that person was and how their belongings came to be on the *Titanic* and then filmed by the underwater camera of Magellan's ROV. Part of the research into this involved examining footage and images of the *Titanic*'s passengers to see if there is any indication as to who owned this remarkable artefact.

At the end of this very secretive expedition, the team gathered for a memorial ceremony where flowers were laid in memory of the 1,500 people who died at this spot more than a century before. The survey ship then turned for home, once again leaving the *Titanic* in peace.

In the meantime, *Freja* returned to the Channel Islands ready for its next expedition. Magellan and partners Atlantic Productions released their new information to a world excited to see the 3D models of *Titanic*, attracting a considerable amount of news and other media coverage, CEO Richard Parkinson being interviewed time and again by TV crews. He described the model as being ten times larger than any other 3D model ever attempted, 'an absolutely one-to-one digital copy, a twin of the *Titanic* in every detail'. In 2023, the company also announced the newest addition to their fleet, the research vessel *Coco*. Named after Richard Parkinson's daughter, the ship was chartered to give the fleet the capability to head anywhere on the planet and burn less fuel while doing so.

Magellan would be involved with the *Titanic* once again in 2023, only this time it was not exploring the wreck itself but involving a rescue mission.

23

COMMERCIAL DIVING WITH *TITAN* (2021-2022)

A NEW COMPANY made the headlines in 2021 when Oceangate announced that they had built several submersibles that were capable of diving to the deep oceans and could, for a price, take anybody willing to pay the money. Already having developed the *Cyclops*, CEO Stockton Rush was thrilled to be able to introduce people to dives on the wreck of the *Titanic*. He said such trips would not only break the rules for diving but be a huge risk that, in his opinion, would mean he would be achieving so much more by disregarding all the red tape and regulations that seemed to tie down every innovative adventurer.

As the world moved into the 2020s, the technology in the submersible world became more sophisticated, meaning that comparing the latest underwater craft to the likes of *Alvin* from the 1960s was like comparing chalk and cheese. The 22ft-long *Titan* weighed just 10.4 tons and was described by Oceangate as a revolutionary carbon fibre and titanium submersible which could go to depths of 13,000ft (4,000 metres), allowing it to access almost 50 per cent of the world's oceans.

The sub resembled a teardrop-shaped sea creature, having a white hull with the company name down the side and a glass viewport at the front, where the crew could sit and look out with a better vantage

Horizon Arctic, mother ship to the *Titan* on the first *Titanic* dives by Oceangate. (Gordon Leggett)

point than any previous underwater craft, which was limited to smaller viewing ports consisting of thick glass to protect the passengers from the extreme pressures pressing down on them. Oceangate developed *Titan* after working for several years with a previous model named *Cyclops*, in which they carried out dives on the wreck of the liner *Andrea Doria*. They drew up plans for an even better version in order to be able to mount an expedition to the *Titanic*.

The difference with their new submersible was that it could carry five people, more than any other undersea vehicle of this nature, seemingly leaving it far ahead of the rest in design and innovation. While Oceangate advertised their services for those wanting to carry out inspections and surveys, the *Titanic* offered a unique way for those with a keen interest in the famous ship to visit the wreck for themselves – for a large amount of money. Their website advertised the 2022 expedition, offering to take visitors for a princely sum, which would allow a single dive to the wreck.

Towed on top of a barge by the offshore supply vessel *Horizon Arctic*, the *Titan* would be taken from the American coast to the *Titanic* wreck site, where the barge would simply tilt and allow the *Titan* to slide into the water. At 305ft long and having a gross weight of 8,269 tons, the *Horizon Arctic* (IMO Number 9732838) was built in 2016 at the Vard Brattvaag shipyard in Norway and was owned by Horizon Maritime. It was originally constructed for the oil industry as a heavy-duty offshore tug/supply vessel, with an ice-strengthened bow for working in the freezing Arctic conditions of the Norwegian and Canadian oilfields. Despite its huge blue hull having a bulbous front that made it look like a metal whale, the ship was perfect for functioning in cold weather climates. The sixty berths on board allowed plenty of room for an expedition team to work with ease while launching a series of underwater vehicles.

In 2021, Oceangate Expeditions chartered *Horizon Arctic* from its owners to be used as their surface support ship, intending that over the next three years the *Titan* would be launched for dozens of private dives, creating footage that could allow scientists to study the marine biology in and around the wreck as well as further map the debris field. The plan was for thousands of photographs to be taken to compare with data from previous expeditions.

One thing Oceangate did insist on was that they were not there to salvage anything from the wreck. Instead, they were offering to take people to see the *Titanic*. In 2023, their website offered the opportunity, for the price of around $250,000 each, to become a member of the expedition team (known as a 'mission specialist'), and work on board the vessel, where training would take place and one dive to the wreck of the *Titanic*. This price did not include travel insurance or the journey to and from the ship. None of this put people off. Some of those who had the chance to go down to the wreck said that it was a remarkable experience and they had no regrets about spending that amount of money for this life-changing event. The expeditions were marketed as a resounding success, with more incredible footage taken of the remains of the wreck and more people than ever able to view *Titanic* up close.

Despite misgivings from people who doubted the ability of Oceangate's Stockton Rush to make the dives happen safely, *Titan* did dive to *Titanic* as planned in 2021 and 2022, and as promised they brought back amazing footage of a wreck that was becoming a very different one to that which Robert Ballard had first looked upon thirty-seven years previously. Oceangate aimed to conduct mapping and photography of the wreck over the space of several years and promised to comply with all NOAA and UNESCO guidelines when visiting the site, with nothing taken from it.

The results the team brought back were pored over by *Titanic* experts and fed into the existing database on the state of decay of the wreck. The video footage alone was in 8K, the highest-ever resolution used on the wreck. It seemed that the *Titan* was performing flawlessly as expected, and the submersible was expected to go back to the site for several more years. While there was still a fascination with *Titanic*, there would be a reason for the expeditions to continue.

However, what the public saw and what was actually going on behind the scenes were two completely different things. Questions were being asked over the legitimacy of the safety of the *Titan*, with debate surrounding the ability of the shape of the hull to deal with the extreme pressures, and there was also concern about the 'cowboy' attitude of Stockton Rush and the fact that none of his company's equipment was certified by anybody, potentially putting lives at risk.

In 2018, Rob McCallum and Stockton Rush had exchanged a number of emails, which were highlighted several years later in news reports regarding McCallum's warning that the *Titan* was not safe to dive in. Rush responded by saying that he was 'tired of industry players who try to use a safety argument to stop innovation', basically dismissing any safety concerns from a man who had already safely led dozens of *Titanic* expeditions with the *Mir* submersibles and by now knew the wreck and the dangers involved inside out.

The *Titan* submersible was a unique shape, as seen in this 3D model. (Tim Samedov)

While Rush's ignorant response to anyone highlighting the dangers of such a blasé approach to deep sea diving got the backs up of many people, technically there was nothing stopping him from simply doing what he wanted with no consequences, as highlighted by the fact that his expeditions were going ahead and people were more than happy to pay a huge amount of money to be a 'mission specialist' on an uncertified submersible.

The fact that *Titan* had so far managed to dive to the *Titanic* with no problems renewed Rush's confidence, and that of his teams, in apparently having proved that the submersible could reach such depths and return safely. Despite interviews in which he showed TV crews that the submersible would literally be bolted shut as passengers entered through the bow dome, then controlled via a messaging service and a remote control that was a replica of what gamers used on a PlayStation, people still signed up to make the journey.

With the next expedition already planned for the following year, what could possibly go wrong?

24

TRAGEDY OF THE *TITAN* (2023)

THE 2012 CENTENARY had the story of the *Titanic* back in the headlines again, as did the release of the Cameron movie in 1997 in the wave of publicity that saw the director become 'King of the world' with eleven Oscars. Nonetheless, nobody expected the *Titanic* to hit the front pages around the world quite as dramatically as it did in the summer of 2023. Oceangate was once again planning a commercial diving expedition, this time using the research vessel *Polar Prince*, an ice-breaking ship 239.5ft long and weighing 2,062 gross tons.

Launched at the Canadian Davie Yards shipyard in Levis in 1959 as the *Sir Humphrey Gilbert*, this vessel was specifically designed for conditions in the frozen seas of the Arctic, operating out of Canadian waters for the Department of Transport Marine Service until three years later, when the ship came under the ownership of the new Canadian Coast Guard.

Having been rebuilt following retirement from active service in 1986, it was given the unusual name of *2001–06* in 2001, still under ownership of the Canadian government, before being sold in 2002 to Norcon Marine Services Ltd, for whom it started its new role as the *Gilbert I*. Again, it did not spend long under that name, Star Line Inc acquiring the vessel a year later, when it became the *Polar Prince*, later coming under ownership of Horizon Maritime Services. It was temporarily renamed *Canada C3* for a high-profile visit to the areas around Canada's three coasts as part of the 150-year anniversary of

For the 2023 expedition, Oceangate used the *Polar Prince* – seen here in 2017 – as mother ship to *Titan*. (Photo – The Interior)

the nation, but was soon after back to being called *Polar Prince* (IMO Number 5329566).

The ship looks like a regular ice patrol ship, with a red hull and a Canadian maple leaf halfway down the hull, a red funnel, white superstructure from midships aft, space on the forward deck to have a large A-frame and a number of control vans anchored to the deck for scientific work to be carried out. As a support vessel, the *Polar Prince* was just what an expedition like this would want.

It was chartered by Oceangate for their 2023 dives to the *Titanic*, and in the early May of that year the now blue-hulled vessel sailed east, with the *Titan* submersible towed behind, ready to make what would be their third expedition to the wreck. With all the previous safety warnings being ignored and many of them not even public knowledge, the expedition set off to conduct the first dives as the press waited for the results and images to be fed back to them.

As I was writing this book, with the expedition of the summer of 2023 still ongoing, a check of the Sky News website had breaking news of a very serious incident. *Titan* had gone down to the wreck of the *Titanic* on Sunday, 18 June, with five people on board: Paul-Henri Nargeolet (a veteran of many previous expeditions), Oceangate

Coast Guard *HC-130* and the French research vessel *L'Atalante* searching in vain for the lost submersible *Titan*. (US Coast Guard photo)

CEO Stockton Rush and three fee-paying passengers, the billionaires Hamish Harding (UK), Shahzada Dawood and his son, Suleman (both Pakistan/UK nationality). One hour and forty-five minutes into the dive, all contact was lost with the submersible. With only ninety-six hours of air in reserve, the race was on to locate the missing *Titan*. As soon as the US Coast Guard had been alerted, a full-scale rescue mission swung into action.

The days dragged painfully on. Reports came in of a banging noise which was possibly the crew signalling for help, but the rescue ships and aircraft searching for the missing sub could not pinpoint where it was coming from, nor if it was even the *Titan*. Oceangate's reputation was quickly in tatters, with previous 'mission specialists' coming forward to give their opinions about the submersible not being safe and the craft itself being made from parts you could order online, such as the video games controller that was used to pilot the vessel. More information just made the story more shocking, the world learning of the fact that the waiver that had to be signed before embarking on the dive mentioned death no fewer than three times. Several people said that, looking back, they did not feel comfortable on board and indeed felt unsafe, a few even cancelling their trip. All this happened while Oceangate's promotion of a safe and reliable submersible was all that ever seemed to be reported back to a world still hungry for more information about the *Titanic*.

In the meantime, more details emerged of the possibility of the five people on board being alive. But although they had originally had almost 100 hours of emergency air as well as rations to keep them alive as ships from every nearby port hastily departed, deploying their sensors and underwater search equipment, each one would take several days to get to the scene. Time was ticking away.

With dozens of organizations and several ships racing to the *Titanic* site, news stations broadcast live from press conferences as eagerly awaited updates were given. It was a full two days before the first rescue ships started to arrive on the scene. Pipe-laying vessel *Deep Energy*, with ROVs on board, was soon joined by the *Skandi Vinland*, Canadian Coast Guard ships *John Cabot* and *Atlantic Merlin*, IFREMER research vessel *L'Atalante* and the veteran of previous *Titanic* expeditions *Horizon Arctic*. Even Magellan was called in to help the rescue mission, although their ROV never left the airport as time was running out and the go-ahead from the United States government was not given in time. Their equipment sat idle at the airport in Jersey, waiting for a military aircraft, until eventually they had to give up any hope of realistically being able to assist in the search.

One by one, the ships took up position in the search area and launched their vehicles, the French having *Victor 6000*, a ROV that could assist with releasing a submersible if trapped, while *Horizon Arctic* had on board the Flyaway Deep Ocean Salvage System

The nose cone from the sunken *Titan* was salvaged and brought ashore just days after the discovery of the wreckage. (US Coast Guard)

(FADOSS), which had the ability to pull the stricken sub back to the surface.

Tuesday turned into Wednesday with no word of contact being made. Noises that were initially thought to be the crew banging for help turned out not to be them. Not since 1912 had so many ships descended on this area, the pressure being on as the time where the air would have run out passed without any word of the *Titan* on the morning of Thursday, 22 June.

That same day, confirmation came of everybody's worst fears. Cameras on the seabed had found what remained of the *Titan* submersible in pieces, around 1,600ft away from the bow of the liner's wreck, on a smooth part of seabed where no *Titanic* remains lay. The announcement was then made that all five crew had perished when the sub imploded four days previously at the start of their dive.

As the following days went by, questions were asked about the safety and competency of Oceangate, and how such a tragedy was allowed to happen despite so many concerns being voiced. Film director James Cameron hit the nail on the head when he stated that both *Titanic* and *Titan* were lost due to unheeded warnings, and both were now lying next to each other over 2 miles down. Days later, the remains of *Titan* were recovered and a major investigation launched. What was not lost on some was the fact that a migrant boat that sank in the Mediterranean a few days before had killed more than 600 people, yet this gained very little media attention compared to a mini-sub full of rich people in close proximity to the world's most famous shipwreck. Stories with any relation to *Titanic* always made the front pages, with much more coverage than the unnamed victims of a sunken fishing vessel called *Adriana*.

The Wallace Hartley monument in Colne town centre, showing flowers left for the crew of *Titan* two weeks after the disaster. (Author)

In the village of Colne in Lancashire, a bust of *Titanic* band leader Wallace Hartley honours the famous hero of the liner – who played on while the ship sank – but in the summer of 2023 a solitary pot containing flowers was left by someone unknown, paying tribute to the loss of the *Titan* and its five crew. The tragedy of the *Titan* was now firmly part of the story of the *Titanic*.

On 28 June 2023, countless news cameras were rolling in St Johns, Newfoundland, as the *Horizon Arctic* brought back the nose cone of the *Titan*, cranes lifting it up for offloading onto the jetty. A tarpaulin covered most of it from the world's eyes, but nevertheless it was final physical confirmation of the fate of the submersible. On 6 July, Oceangate suspended all explorations, their website having a simple black screen with a very short explanation. Only time will tell if the fallout from the *Titan* disaster has international implications on home-made submarines and commercial deep-sea diving, but what is for sure is that this was one expedition to *Titanic* that will never be forgotten.

25

THE DIVES MUST GO ON (2024)

A YEAR PASSED from the loss of the *Titan*, with the investigation still ongoing, when it was announced that dives to the *Titanic* would continue. The *Dino Chouest* was to sail to the wreck site to conduct a comprehensive survey of the area for RMS Titanic Inc. Tragically, this was meant to have been led by Paul-Henri Nargeolet on what would be the company's ninth expedition to the wreck.

The *Dino Chouest* was launched as an offshore supply vessel in 2009 from the North American Shipbuilding yard in Larose, Louisiana, and was owned by Edison Chouest Offshore (ECO). Weighing 5,993 gross tons, the ship was 348ft long, with a distinct red hull that made it recognizable from afar. Most of the work on board took place in the front half of the vessel, allowing anything that required shipping, launching or work carrying out to be done on the aft section. Supplying the majority of Gulf of Mexico deep-water operations with support vessels of different kinds, ECO has been established since 1960.

On 12 July 2024, the *Dino Chouest* sailed from Providence, Rhode Island, heading to the wreck of the *Titanic* in a blaze of publicity, being the first expedition to the site since the previous year's tragedy. Their mission was to take high-resolution photographs using ROVs to preserve the state of the wreck digitally, comparing the new images with those taken fourteen years before on RMS Titanic Inc's last expedition. A survey was also to be made of the wireless room area. Led by David

A visit by the author to the *Titanic* artefacts in Buena Park, California, in 2016. (Author)

Gallo, a veteran of Woods Hole for over thirty years, and Troy Launay, who was on the 1998 expedition, they aimed to seek ways to preserve the *Titanic* in every way possible. Gallo was keen to actually dive the wreck, as he had only previously visited it using ROVs.

The team also wanted to lay a plaque to Paul-Henri Nargeolet on the wreck, a year after his loss in the *Titan*. As the final dives were completed, the plaque was placed on the wreck, the final resting place of the explorer and former French Navy commander who became known as 'Mr Titanic'.

At the same time as the *Dino Chouest* was getting ready to sail, Larry Connor and Patrick Lahey were announcing their own visit to the *Titanic* site using Triton Submarines, the company that had previously visited the wreck in 2019. Using a submersible named *Triton 4000/2 Abyssal Explorer*, Connor had founded Triton in 2008. The two explorers had already been to the Mariana Trench in 2021 and wanted to prove that commercial diving on the wreck of the *Titanic* was indeed safe despite the *Titan* disaster. This led to a barrage of comments on social media that ridiculed any further attempt at risking lives to go to see a shipwreck that had already been visited, salvaged, mapped, photographed and scanned numerous times. By now, many were calling for the *Titanic* to be left in peace, while others just wanted an end to be put to the dives, which were seen as being a rich person's plaything.

The Triton website advertised the submersible as 'the only acrylic-hulled submersible commercially certified for dives in excess of 13,000 ft'. The focus here was on the word 'certified', which was something that *Titan* never was. The company was also highlighting their safety features, their launch procedures and the fact that the dive would take place the second the submersible was launched, rather than wasting precious time bobbing around on the surface. They called this a 'Direct Dive'; as soon as the sub is released, it is underwater and heading off to work. Visually, the sub looks like one of the tourist craft that frequent places like the Red Sea, a glass sphere with two people sat in pilot chairs either side of each other, with a view all around. A flap on each side of the submersible slowly extends outwards, like wings, with lights shining forward, lighting the way for those aboard to get up close to the seabed. All this is in a vessel just 14.6ft in length and weighing only 12 tons, powered by four thrusters on an emergency 24V supply battery. However, with the *Titan* tragedy so fresh in the minds of people, only time will tell if commercial dives to this legendary shipwreck will carry on for much longer.

In September 2024, after the RMS Titanic Inc expedition had returned to dry land, they released new footage of the wreck showing part of the railing on the port bow was now missing. After over a century of it being in place (and possibly being side-swiped by ROVs and submersibles), this small piece of the ship now lays in the mud below. Despite the fact that these guardrails were designed to detach if needed, the damage still provoked shock amongst researchers and *Titanic* fans alike, creating a talking point for many weeks thereafter. Whether or not the guardrail was meant to detach, the sight of the ship slowly deteriorating is sad to see.

David Concannon continued to be involved in the *Titanic* expeditions after he had organized the 2000 trip. He has now dived the *Titanic* five times and been on the expeditions that took place in 2003, 2005, 2021 and 2022. He has represented and acted as an advisor to RMS Titanic Inc, James Cameron, DOE, Oceangate, Atlantic Productions and various other private-sector organizations relating to issues surrounding the *Titanic* wreck site, and by 2024 he was representing no less than three contractors on that year's surveys.

He had a lucky escape in 2023, when he was meant to be the subject matter expert diving in *Titan* with Oceangate on the fatal dive. He had to cancel his taking part just thirty-six hours before the vessel

One of many models of the *Titanic* wreck that are displayed around the world. This one was exhibited in Southampton in 2013. (Author)

departed from St Johns. Paul-Henri Nargeolet took Concannon's seat in the submersible and never returned. Having already visited the wreck five times in various expeditions, Concannon has also given up his seat a further seven times to people so they could have the opportunity to see the wreck for themselves. When asked if he would go back to the wreck of the *Titanic*, he replied: 'No, but the reality is I always get asked to go and I sometimes have a hard time saying no.'

Such is the attraction that *Titanic* has to people, it is very difficult not to pass up an opportunity to be involved in these historic expeditions and become a part of the story.

Rob McCallum of Deep Ocean Exploration has carried out a huge number of high-profile expeditions around the world's oceans. Since his last visit to the *Titanic* in 2005, he has organized trips such as The Five Deeps Expedition between 2018 and 2020, the Ring of

The bow of the *Titanic* wreck has become the most iconic image of any expedition. This shot is from the 2003 dives. (NOAA)

Fire in 2020–2021, Challenger ANZAC in 2021, a second Ring of Fire expedition from 2021–2022 and several down to the wreck of the *Bismarck*. These were world-record and world-first descents to the deepest points of the Atlantic, Pacific, Indian, Arctic and Southern oceans, along with the deepest point in each of the world's four 10,000-metre-plus trenches, the Wallaby Fracture Zone, San Cristobal Trench (8,483m), Santa Cruz Trench (9,142m) and New Hebrides Trench (7,794m). These DOE expeditions have explored all of the world's 10,000m-plus trenches and include the Horizon Deep (second-deepest on Earth), Philippines Trench (third-deepest), Calypso (deepest point of the Mediterranean) and the Suakin Trough (deepest point of the Red Sea).

It has not just been the *Mir* submersibles that he has hired for his expeditions. Dozens of other dives have been conducted in the *Deep Rover 1* and *2*, *Deep Challenge* for James Cameron as well as a number of submersible vehicles for Triton.

The *Nadir* at sea as the *Alucia*, seen here off Rotterdam, Netherlands, in 2021. (Hans Esveldt)

Hundreds of scientists and explorers have now taken advantage of these expeditions, it being easier to simply hire his team than to organize it themselves. The search for shipwrecks and hidden history has also seen the documenting and finding of the USS *Johnston* and USS *Samuel B. Roberts*, sunk in the Second World War; the 'Sammy B' being the deepest shipwreck ever located. In 2011, DOE were called upon to help search for the remains of Air France flight 447, as was the *Nautile*, but it was McCallum's team that located the wreckage and recovered vital evidence for investigation teams that led to the cause of the crash being found. Another expedition was to the French submarine *Minerve*, which had been found recently after vanishing in 1968 with the loss of all its crew.

Rob McCallum could not stay quiet regarding the loss of the *Titan*. He had attempted to persuade Stockton Rush not to operate his

The MV *Alucia* (formerly *Nadir*) in the Russian port of St Petersburg in February 2019. (Adog)

submersibles without the right classifications, tests and certifications. He was concerned that Oceangate were not operating to the correct standards, and were in effect putting the lives of themselves and their clients at risk. Needless to say, he was soon proved correct when *Titan* was lost in June 2023.

At the time of writing, McCallum is on the board of the Nekton Foundation, a charity based in the UK that works towards the acceleration of scientific exploration of the seas and oceans. He is also chairman of its Expedition Committee responsible for operations at sea, that have been confirmed as having resulted in the discovery of The Rariphotic Zone and Trapping Zone, two new ecosystems that are the largest found on the planet in decades. A huge area is now protected as a result of these expeditions, thanks to the work his organisation has carried out. In April 2023, the Nekton Foundation launched the Ocean Census, the largest programme of its kind in history, to discover new ocean life and record it in numerous expeditions that are still ongoing today. Documentary makers are still hiring his team and ships to make incredible and popular award-winning shows, such as *Blue Planet II* and *Frozen Planet*, showing amazing new footage of underwater life that has never before been broadcast, providing information to universities, film crews and influential people worldwide. This work has included taking Prince Albert II of Monaco down to the Calypso Deep in the Mediterranean and the former Palauan president, Tommy Remengesau, to the deep ocean to view the Palau Trench, some 1,000km east of the Philippines, huge milestones in their nations' history.

Ocean exploration shows no sign of diminishing, but everyone who descends to the depths has to be incredibly careful. The sea is a cruel mistress, and as we have seen, whether it is 1912 or 2023, it takes no prisoners.

EPILOGUE

THE *TITANIC* RESTED in peace for seventy-three silent years, an undisturbed tomb to some 1,500 lost souls. When Robert Ballard located the wreck in 1985, there was an element of reflection, respect and study involved, with no artefacts being taken and none of the wreck being touched. Subsequent expeditions showed that cameras could be deployed to a shipwreck of this magnitude while treating it with respect.

Over the four decades since the discovery, there has been an unhealthy obsession with diving the wreck 'for scientific purposes', when all that was actually being done was expedition teams being given a free-for-all on taking artefacts and selling stories, photographs and TV rights. Very little real surveying was done for the millions of dollars being spent on dive after dive in manned craft, putting lives at risk for the same photographs that had already been seen countless times in hundreds of books. It was only when James Cameron gently entered the wreck and got the first images of the Turkish baths and some of the internal rooms that we finally got some footage that did not disturb the wreck and actually added something new to the *Titanic* story. It remains to be seen just how many more times the wreck can be filmed using ever higher-definition images, how much more mapping and scanning can be done, while 'monitoring deterioration' of the liner.

The recovery of thousands of *Titanic* artefacts was always going to be a controversial decision; one side accused them of grave robbing, while the other claimed they were the saviours of historical items. But could the latter excuse be given for the selling of the coal from the wreck? Is it any different from trudging the fields around Lockerbie and selling pieces of aircraft wreckage on eBay to a collector?

Philip Littlejohn died in 2014 after spending his life researching his grandfather Alexander Littlejohn, who had survived the sinking. The opportunity to be the first family member of anybody on board *Titanic* to visit the wreck was one that he was glad he took. His later book on the story of First-Class Steward Littlejohn was well received by people within the *Titanic* community; both Alexander's and Philip's legacies live on.

My own *Titanic* collection consisted largely of books and DVDs, but some extremely tasteless items have appeared on the market, poking fun at tragedy, all just to make a quick few pounds. The wreck of the *Titanic* will eventually collapse, like so many wrecks around the world, and there will be nothing left but a pile of rusted metal pieces.

My own journey into the story of the *Titanic* began in 1991, when I first watched the movie *Raise the Titanic*. This spark led me to write more than twenty books on history and shipwrecks, including writing *RMS Titanic: The Bridlington Connections*, highlighting the links the ship had to my home town. This led to a plaque being placed at the local theatre to commemorate Wallace Hartley, the band leader who played on until the end and made the ultimate sacrifice, as did all his fellow musicians. In 1997, I attended the annual British Titanic Society convention in Southampton, where I met expert Steve Rigby, one of the original members of the group. I was saddened when I heard that he had passed away, but I am glad that Steve had managed to carry out his lifelong ambition to visit the wreck. He was a great guy, and for the kindness he showed me that year, when I was just a lad, I have dedicated this book to his memory.

After the disaster of the *Titan*, newspapers were full of questions about why manned submersibles were still being used to dive the

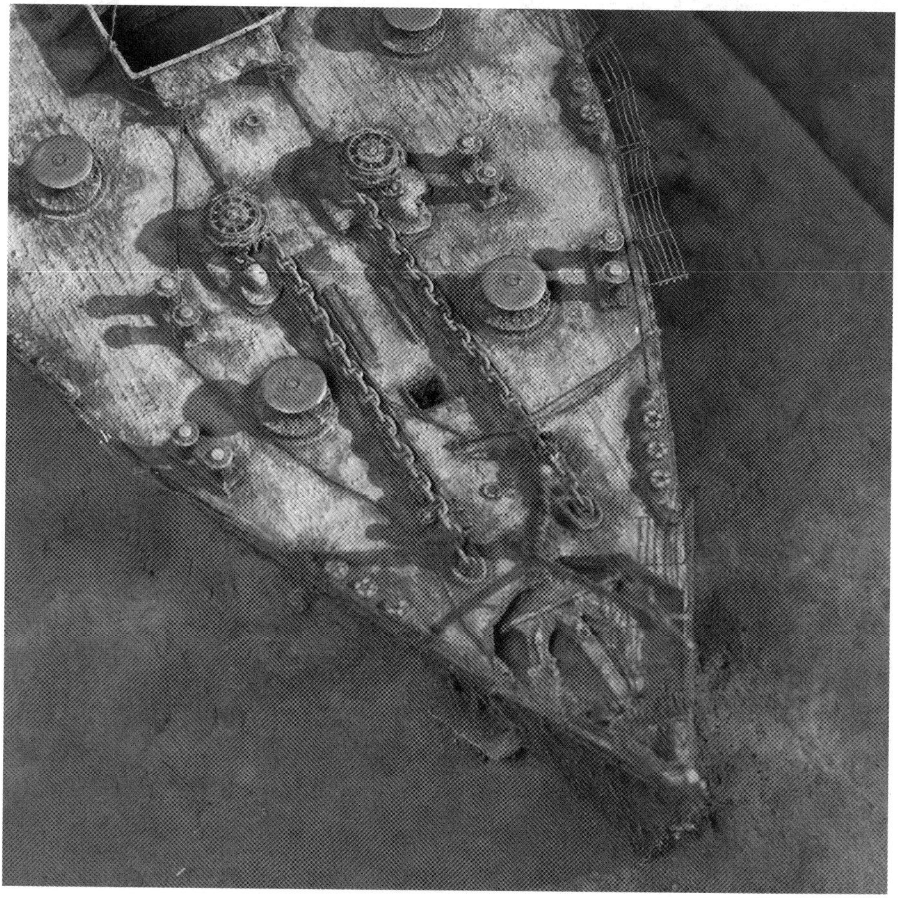

Above and opposite: Stuart Williamson's model of the *Titanic* wreck. (Stuart Williamson)

wreck, laying so far down, when remotely operated cameras could do the same job, with a vastly reduced risk to life and limb. It may have made many people think twice about stepping on board a commercial submersible as the mangled remains of the *Titan* were hoisted on board a recovery ship in the glare of TV news cameras. For the first time since the release of the 1997 movie, the *Titanic* was back on the front page of newspapers. People's fascination regarding the loss of the world's most famous liner – their longing for more detail and further updates – shows no sign of abating, with ever more stories keeping coming from explorations of the wreck.

There are now no living survivors of the *Titanic*, the last one being Millvina Dean, who died in 2009 on the anniversary of the ship's launch. By coincidence, her brother, Bert – also a survivor – had died on the eightieth anniversary of the ship's sinking. There is nobody left alive who has seen *Titanic* in all its glory, sailing from Belfast or Southampton, ploughing the waves of the Solent or steaming into the night towards its fate. As for the expedition crews, George Tulloch died of cancer just a few years after his dives, Paul-Henri Nargeolet was lost in the *Titan* implosion and Jack Grimm passed away in 1998. But the *Titanic* story lives on through thousands of books and documentaries, over twenty movies and TV dramas, and of course the exhibitions, museums and 5,500 salvaged items that have been brought up from the wreck.

In February 2016, my wife and I were married in Southampton. The story of the *Titanic* has been a huge part of our life, so it was only fitting that on our honeymoon, after we had spent a week in San Francisco, we headed to Long Beach to spend the second week on board the *Queen Mary*, the closest we will now ever get to the grandeur of the classic days of the ocean liners. During our time on board there was an exhibition of *Titanic* artefacts in nearby Buena Park, and of course we could not resist going along. Despite the controversy of their recovery, they are cared for and displayed in a tasteful way, and it was fascinating to see them. The *Titanic* was (and still is) an important part of history; since its loss, so many things have changed, not least nautical safety and of course the dreaded class system.

This was the third time I had seen the *Titanic* artefacts. The first time was in the Science Museum in 2003 and the second time at the O2 Arena in London a few years later. Each time, I am mesmerised by the stories that come with them and to learn of just how they were brought from the seabed under such extreme conditions.

The man who discovered the wreck, Robert Ballard, went on to promote deep-ocean exploration and history by finding numerous other historic wrecks, and even had a go at finding Amelia Earhart. He will always be the one person who inspired me as a child to go on to study history and shipwrecks, just as he inspired many thousands of others around the world and continues to do so today.

There are reportedly a staggering three million shipwrecks around the world. *Titanic* is just one of them, yet there is more focus on this one shipwreck than the thousands of others that can tell us just as much about this era. The exploration of shipwrecks has led to academic studies of periods of our history that have found more new evidence than many land-based archaeological sites – wrecks such as the *Mary Rose* (Tudor), the unknown wreck off Alderney (Elizabethan), HMS *Invincible* (Georgian) and CSS *Hunley* (American Civil War), to name just a few. Many of these wrecks are raised and preserved in museums so that we can study and appreciate their period. Contrary to popular belief, the *Titanic* cannot tell us much that we don't already know.

The *Mir 2* dive during the 2005 expedition. (Heidi and Joe Porter/ *Wreckdiving* magazine)

There are many currently undiscovered wrecks that deserve our attention. There's the *Bonhomme Richard*, the famous warship captained by John Paul Jones in 1779; the liner *Waratah*, missing with all hands in 1909 and never seen again; the USS *Cyclops*, which led to the area known as the Bermuda Triangle becoming a notorious stretch of ocean; and of course the missing aircraft carrying Amelia Earhart and her navigator, Fred Noonan. We now have explorers such as David Mearns, who has found the wrecks of HMS *Hood*, the *Derbyshire* and HMAS *Sydney*, and the diver Mensun Bound, who located the wreck of Shackleton's *Endurance* in 2022. With so many more shipwrecks to choose from, we can learn much about other ways of life at sea as the years progress. There will be other shipwrecks that hit the headlines and make people research and dive them, but will any lead to so many movies, expeditions, historical societies and TV documentaries as did the *Titanic*? As the years go by, with the *Titanic* wreck now being on the edge of serious deterioration, we can only watch as the remains of this once-proud ship fade away to a rusting heap of metal. Soon, even that will be gone.

While ever there is passion for the deep sea and exploration, there will be people determined to solve the mysteries of the oceans. With the wreck of the *Titanic* having been found and explored so extensively, is it worth continuing to visit a ship so deep when so many other missing ships still have their own stories to be told? It can only be hoped that the search for these ships will garner the same amount of attention as has been given to the *Titanic*.

ACKNOWLEDGEMENTS

THIS BOOK WOULD not have been possible without the brilliant people who help me whenever I run a project. I have a lot of people to thank, starting with my family and going all around the world to those who reply to my requests, emails, letters and social media posts. Specifically, I would like to say a special thanks to the following people and organizations that were instrumental in me completing this book:

Sue Miller, the sister of *Titanic* expert Steve Rigby, who allowed me to use her brother's story and photos in a blog post online before she granted me permission to tell the story here. Steve was a brilliant bloke; for his kindness shown to me when I was just 16 years old at the British Titanic Society convention, I now dedicate this book to his memory.

David Hutchings, who has written several fantastic books on ocean liners, including a number on the *Titanic*, and who was involved in the first Big Piece expedition in 1996. He talked me through what it was like to be there when history was being made, and allowed me to use his vast collection of photos, documents and information that he collected on board the *Royal Majesty*.

Caroline Graham, who told me what it was like to be on board as a journalist, interviewing those making the dives.

Rob McCallum, for the detail that he allowed me to see regarding the expeditions that he organized over the years and the incredible insight into the workings behind these complex journeys.

David Concannon, for his story about the dives to *Titanic* that he carried out over the years.

Richie Kohler, for not only his story on how he came to be on *Titanic*, but also for his marvellous four-series *Deep Sea Detectives*, which kept me entertained for hours and highlighted some of the many shipwrecks around the world that would otherwise not receive any attention.

Stuart Williamson, for his amazing artwork and permission to use some of it for this book. His *Britannic* at sea and underwater paintings have both hung on my wall for the last twenty years and are amongst my favourite pieces of art.

Scott Caldwell, for allowing me to see his White Star items, including relics salvaged from another liner, the *Arabic*.

The National Oceanic and Atmospheric Administration, for allowing me to use their images and information and for the fantastic work they do on our world's oceans. Keep up the amazing work!

Triton Submarines LLC, for their response to my request for information.

I contacted many organizations and people involved in the dives to the *Titanic* over the years. The first reply I received was from Dr Robert Ballard, so a special thanks to him not only for his response but for inspiring me over the years to study shipwrecks and history. It really has changed my life.

BIBLIOGRAPHY

'3 Other Submersibles Visiting Titanic Almost Suffered The Same Fate As Titan', 15 June 2023, retrieved from CBS News

Ballard, R.D., *The Discovery of the Titanic* (1987)

Ballard, R.D., *Return to Titanic – A New Look at the World's Most Famous Ship* (2004)

Ballard, R.D., *Into the Deep – A Memoir From the Man Who Found Titanic* (2021)

Ballard, R.D. & Michel, J.L., *The RMS Titanic 1985 Discovery Expedition* (1985)

Best, A.I., *et al.*, 'Geotechnical Investigation of the Titanic Wreck Site', *Marine Georesources and Geotechnology* (2000)

Dromgoole, S., 'The International Agreement for the Protection of the Titanic: Problems and Prospects', *Ocean Development and International Law* (2006)

Garzke, W.H. *et al.*, 'A Marine Forensic Analysis of the RMS Titanic' (n.d.)

Graham, C., 'My Dive To Titanic', *The Mail on Sunday* (19 September 1999)

Hoffman, W. & Grimm, J., *Beyond Reach: The Search for the Titanic* (1982)

McCarty, J.H. & Foecke, T., 'Microscopic Analysis of Metal Recovered from the Wreck of RMS Titanic', *Microscopy Today* (2007), pp.6–10

McCaughan, M., 'National Maritime Museum, Reading the Relics: Titanic Culture and The Wreck of the Titanic Exhibit', *Material History Review* 43 (2007)

Nesmeyanov, E., *The Titanic Expeditions* (2021)

Salazar, M. & Little, B., 'Review – Rusticle Formation on the RMS Titanic and the Potential Influence on Oceanography' (2017)

Sanchez-Porro, C., *et al*., 'Halomonas titanicae sp. nov., a halophilic bacterium isolated from the RMS Titanic', *International Journal of Systematic and Evolutionary Microbiology* (2010), pp.2768–74